Contents

C000148022

Contents

Introduction

A company counselling service? The manager as counsellor? To some, this will sound far-fetched even for today. Management has certainly changed. Long ago, managers gave orders. Next, managers still gave orders but gave them politely and with explanations. That method in turn ceased to work wherever technology and administration systems became more complicated and subordinates were increasingly liable to know more of particular aspects of the work than the manager did. Many modern managers are much more, for example, negotiators and bargainers and builders of useful networks than order-givers. But counsellors?

The objections are easily listed. Isn't counselling for the sick? Can't normal people manage their own problems? If you mean listening, don't managers do that anyway? Aren't managers busy enough already? Isn't it enough to offer health and safety, equal opportunity, maternity leave, longer and longer holidays, appraisal and training? What more do they want? Where does any manager today find the time? When are we supposed to get some work done and make a few profits?

Faced with such reasonable inquiries, anyone writing a book about counselling in the workplace, whether it is to be supplied by the manager or by external counsellors, had better provide a convincing cost-benefit analysis for such a service. And yet neither the idea of counselling in the workplace nor the belief that it benefits the organisation are new.

During the late 1920s the Western Electric Company (USA) began, at its Hawthorne plant, the series of experiments in working conditions and methods of supervision which became famous as the Hawthorne Experiments.[1] One outcome of the experiments was the setting up of a counselling service staffed by external consultants offering an opportunity for confidential discussion of personal concerns. The service was introduced in the belief that an individual's worries, from whatever source they arose, were likely to impede his or her work performance and could often be alleviated by counselling. Perhaps the strongest evidence of its effectiveness in reducing stress was provided by the unions, whose officials came to object that employees receiving counselling lost their commitment to union causes!

■ The extent of counselling at work

In the UK redundancy counselling is now widely accepted, linked particularly with the loss of executive jobs. The shake out of jobs in manufacturing, which continues today, began with blue collar jobs in the sixties. From the early seventies it began to hit executive levels and companies started to ease the pain by providing redundancy counselling. The service offered may include financial advice and vocational guidance, but also always includes counselling to help the individual over the shock of major unexpected change.

Although usually offered first to managers, more and more companies have extended this help to all employees. A 1989 survey of 500 companies by Pauline Hyde and Associates[2] found 67 per cent using redundancy counselling compared with 48 per cent five years ago, while 56 per cent had extended the service to supervisors, clerical workers and the hourly paid. Another report published in 1989[3] described the counselling services offered in over 50 organisations. Around 30 per cent of the companies were providing a service where employees had direct access to an independent counsellor. Some 40 per cent provided a service where counselling was available either through counsellors with other duties (for example, line managers, personnel, training, welfare and occupational health specialists) or through contracted external counsellors. The remaining 30 per cent of organisations described services for specific reasons such as career counselling,[3] management development,[1] redundancy,[2] AIDS,[2] alcohol abuse,[3] relocation,[1] violence or armed raids[2] and stress.[2]

Curiously, authors Linda Hoskinson and Michael Reddy found the organisations generally 'bashful' about admitting that they ran a counselling service even when they were investing quite heavily in one. The bashfulness appeared linked to an awareness that counselling is still seen by many people as a service for the sick. They comment that companies need to emphasise that counselling is for healthy people with distracting problems and not only for the sick needing treatment. They found that, although over 70 per cent of the problems presented to counsellors seemed to be 'personal', employers were unanimous that all anxieties from whatever source could detract from efficiency at work and therefore needed to be tackled. All in all they noted a growing awareness in many companies of the need to relate physical and mental health and welfare policies and a recognition that, in this holistic approach, counselling services made an important contribution. Early fears that the cost of such services would escalate out of control had not been realised and confidence in their value and cost-effectiveness was growing. Most importantly, the service has contributed to the retention of valued employees at a time when skilled staff are increasingly scarce.

The consultants Drake Beam Morin[4] surveyed 184 major UK companies (between them employing some 15 million people) and found 84 per cent were offering redundancy counselling to senior executives. Out of the 84 per cent, 43 per cent also offered the service to clerical workers. And although the services were more usual in larger companies than in small, many smaller firms helped staff in this way. (The figures were 89 per cent of companies employing over 10,000 and 79 per cent of those with fewer than 250 staff.)

The services were initially introduced to alleviate the consequences of redundancies and cutbacks (95 per cent of companies); reorganisations and mergers (77 per cent); 'personal chemistry' problems (56 per cent); and career plateau counselling (49 per cent). Not surprisingly, many services were introduced in the period when redundancies peaked, particularly in the oil, gas and energy industries and in manufacturing, engineering and construction industries. More recently the growth has been in the service industries. Drake Beam Morin comment that shop floor and clerical workers are still relatively poorly provided for, and there still seems very little help available for those in professional services.

The CBI has called for positive health promotion initiatives to counteract some of the problems underlying absenteeism which it estimates cost the British economy £5 billion a year.[5] These include work related stress, drink problems and family responsibilities. Counselling is among the measures which could alleviate these conditions.

Among the firms with household names which provide staff counselling services are Whitbreads and Marks and Spencer. Whitbreads runs a three-tier service, including a phone-in system, basic counselling and a referral service of individual counselling for senior staff. Marks and Spencer sends staff on external courses to learn counselling skills and also refers individuals to external counsellors.

■ The Post Office service

One example of a service industry which has recently introduced a counselling service is the Post Office.[6] The idea was first mooted in 1984 by the then Chief Medical Officer Dr Michael McDonald. Faced with a situation in which psychological problems formed the second highest reason for medical retirement, he set up a working party to consider the need for stress counselling. Although the nursing and welfare services already offered first-line counselling, something more specialised seemed required to deal with 'more complex and deep-seated psychological problems' including alcoholism, drug abuse and stress reactions. A three-year pilot project, described by the Post Office as a 'revolutionary new approach to caring for people at work which we believe could set the scene for occupational health in the twenty-first century', was introduced in September 1986. Initially, two counsellors were employed, based in Leeds and Manchester. Subsequently, two part-time counsellors began work in Northern Ireland.

In introducing its specialist counselling service, the Post Office had to accept firstly that the organisation itself could be causing stress and secondly, that such stress needed to be externally evaluated. The organisation had indeed undergone major and rapid change resulting from privatisation and restructuring and the introduction of new technology. Many staff had been put under great strain and had experienced considerable stress and suffered stress related conditions. They needed professional help given with an absolute guarantee of professional confidentiality. In its absence sickness, absenteeism and staff turnover were rising. Thus both humanitarian principles and a belief that the service could help stabilise the workforce underlay the decision to introduce the service.

It was introduced with open access and the counsellors saw 353 clients in the first 22 months. The main categories of problems discussed were mental health and stress; anxiety and depression; relationship problems and marital stress. Twenty-five per cent of clients had considered suicide.

Confidentiality was seen as a key issue. The service was, after all, provided by the organisation and intended to benefit the organisation as well as the individual, a circumstance which imposed a dual loyalty upon the counsellors. The potential for conflict was recognised and the possibility of conflicts of interest was tackled by the counsellors defining the boundaries of confidentiality with their clients at the outset of counselling. Additionally, it was agreed that any feedback to management must be in the client's interest and must be made with the client's express permission. Without that permission, the counsellors would not report.

■ Training in counselling

By whatever name it is called, the value of counselling is increasingly recognised and the skills of counselling are increasingly taught on many management training courses. The Institute of Directors, not noted for a soft-headed approach to business, runs a course called 'Leadership in the 1990s' which includes learning to listen, directive and non-directive techniques, and questioning as important tools for the leader in charge of groups undergoing rapid change or looking after teams of 'knowledge' workers. Another Institute of Directors course covers understanding barriers to change; recognising patterns of response to change; techniques and personal skills for handling transitional periods and strategies to gain acceptance. These are the strategies of influencing and persuading; developing consensus and common ground; joint problem-solving; negotiating change and developing the communication structure. A course on negotiating skills and techniques includes sessions on handling conflict, frustration, stress and pressure, and identifying and dealing with individual needs. A selected list of the organisations offering training in counselling appears in Appendix IV.

So counselling, whether or not it is given open acknowledgement, is certainly already widely recognised and used as a legitimate tool of management. Often introduced to salve the wounds of dramatic change, it has stayed as a valuable service for today's staff and today's work environment. Chapters 1–4 explore the influences in work and the wider community which have given work counselling increased significance today and set out the framework within which the skills discussed later in the book need to be exercised. These are discussed in Chapters 5–13, while Chapter 14 discusses measures the organisation can take to mitigate the adverse effect on staff of rapid adaptation to new circumstances.

■ References

1. Roethlisberger, F.J. and Dickson, W.J., *Management and the Worker*, Harvard Press, 1939.
2. *The Growth and Importance of Outplacement Counselling in the UK in 1989*, a Mori Poll commissioned by Pauline Hyde and Associates, quoted in the *Sunday Times*, 22 October 1989.
3. Hoskinson, L. and Reddy, M., *Counselling Services in UK Organisations*, Independent Counselling Advisory Services (ICAS),1989.
4. *Outpatient Practices of Major Companies in the UK*, paper produced by Drake Beam Morin and presented at Lloyds of London in November 1989.
5. *Managing for Attendance*, CBI,1989.
6. Allinson, T. Cooper, C. and Reynolds, P., 'Stress counselling in the workplace', *The Psychologist*, September 1989.

1· The Changing Workforce

■ Summary

Britain's population structure is changing so that we face a declining number of young people and a large increase in numbers of people aged over 65. An increasing proportion of young people are staying in further and higher education while smaller families mean that more and more women in middle life are available to enter employment. Increasing numbers of people are living alone or with just one other person. The work force of the future will be older and better educated than now and will include many more women. Many will expect work to provide the companionship and interest once expected from home.

These demographic changes are already having a major impact on relationships between men and women, both at work and in the home. Employers are having to come to terms with the differing motivation of men and women and with employees' inescapable domestic responsibilities.

The changes are welcomed by many but those who were happy with the traditional roles of men and women and the traditional division of work from home are adjusting painfully. Counselling is one of the services which may ease this readjustment.

Let us start with the personal implications of demographic change. For very many reasons the birth rate in the developed world has been falling steadily for some decades.

Table 1.1 *Population projections for the UK, Germany and France*

Country	Present population (1986)	Birth rate	Population in year 2000	Population in year 2025
UK	56,763,000	13.3	58,859,000	60,015,000
Germany	61,066,000	10.2	60,484,000	51,140,000
France	55,394,000	14.1	57,789,000	58,152,000

Source: Social Trends 19, HMSO

Belgium is expected to drop in population by nearly one million by 2025, Denmark by half a million, Germany by ten million, the Irish Republic by 300,000 (despite a birth rate of 17.4) and Italy by six million. The number of children in the European community under the age of 15 has decreased from 72 million in 1965 to 64 million in 1985 and is expected to fall further to 49 million in 2025. The number of elderly persons (over the age of 65) on the other hand has increased from 32 million in 1965 to 43 million in 1985 and is expected to reach 64 million by 2025.[1]

The UK population (currently 57 million) is expected to increase by three million by 2025. But the growth is differently distributed between the age cohorts.

Table 1.2 *UK population in millions*

Year	Age range				
	0 - 14	15 - 29	30 - 59	60 - 74	75+
1991	10.8	13.5	20.8	8.0	3.8
2025	11.2	11.2	22.4	10.1	5.3

Source: Office of Population Censuses and Surveys – 1985-based projections

While the population aged 30 upwards will grow by over five million, the population aged 0–29 (which will largely determine the future population growth) will decline, it is projected, by nearly two million.

■ Changes in family life

Related to this changing structure are other situations reflecting great changes in family life. The number of people living alone is steadily rising; in 1961 one person in eight lived alone; in 1987, one in four. It is estimated that by 2001, out of 23.3 million households, nearly one third (7.1 million) will consist of one person only. While many of these single households will be made up of older people (3.9 million aged 60 plus), the one person households of those aged 15–60 will also increase from 2.1 million in 1987 to 3.2 million in 2001.

Many others live with just one other person. For 25 years, just under a third of households have consisted of only two people. These include cohabiting couples, parent–child pairs and childless married couples. But marriage is in overall decline. Indeed there are signs that formal marriage is becoming a cult institution, practised by a declining, though optimistic, proportion of the population.

Table 1.3 *UK marriage trends*

Year	Total population	Total number of marriages	Percentage of marriages as remarriages
1961	52,800,000	397,000	14
1987	56,900,000	398,000	35

Source: Social Trends 19, HMSO

Among families with dependent children the number of lone parents is rising, forming 2.5 per cent of all households in 1961 and rising to 4.7 per cent in 1987. Of such households, 80 per cent are headed by women.

Figures such as these have important implications for employees' mental health. An increasing number of people at work have home lives characterised by solitude or by one important relationship. Whether they value or deplore their state, they are likely to have limited opportunities to resolve the tensions of the working day in discussions at home. Couples may be sustained by the high quality of their relationship but equally severely damaged if that relationship deteriorates. While fewer adults are engaged in child rearing, and those who are are occupied for a shorter number of years, an increasing number are becoming unexpectedly responsible for frail and ageing parents and relatives. These relationships may well be loving but they become, with time, increasingly unlikely to provide a home life where rest, relaxation and recuperation can be taken for granted.

There are some other implications in these figures. Among the reasons for deciding not to have children are the sacrifices in income and standard of living which even one child represents for a dual income couple. Additionally, there is the inevitable setback in the prospects for a mother with career ambitions and the curtailment of shared interests outside the home. Couples who embark on a family are more or less consciously aware of such considerations, so that a decision to leave the wealthy ranks of the DINKS (Double Income No Kids) and have a child becomes a positive preference for alternative benefits.

■ Precious babies

The one or two children in today's small families are thus the focus of much attention and concern. They are helped and expected to do well, to value themselves and, increasingly, to seek a good education and qualifications and worthwhile careers. These expectations apply to girls as well as boys and women now make up over 40 per cent of UK graduates. So the young people coming into employment are likely to be older, better qualified and with higher expectations than previous generations. They are likely to invest more of themselves in their work and to look for more than a pay packet and tolerable working conditions. A job will have to bring mental stimulation, compatible colleagues and a sense of contributing to a worthwhile enterprise.

There is great potential in such commitment, but also plenty of opportunity for mutual disenchantment. Complex modern jobs are not mastered overnight and even much sought-after graduates cannot easily be spared a slow and tedious period of climbing to working competence. On the other hand, the perks they receive can startle their middle management supervisors who came up the hard way while their attitudes towards employment, often emphasising concern for personal advancement rather than company needs, may well irritate and affront.

■ Effect of extending education

The present trend towards extended education and delayed entry into employment is expected to continue: indeed, in this respect, Britain still has far to go to catch up with countries such as Denmark and Germany. The National Economic Development Commission[2] has summarised the effect on the UK labour force in Table 1.4.

Table 1.4 *Age structure of the UK workforce*

Age	Percentage from 1987 to 1995
16–19	–23
20–24	–17
25–34	+16
35–44	+4
45–59	+15
60–64	–3
65+	–25

Source: NEDO Training Commission

■ More women at work

Another effect of the changes in population structure is the increasing number of women now available for employment. Smaller families (or no family) mean less time taken off work to bear and rear children, while better education and career guidance mean, for many, higher work expectations and less satisfaction with a mainly domestic role.

Department of Employment figures predict a growth in the workforce of one million between now and the year 2000 (from 27.6 million to 28.6 million). But 90 per cent of these extra workers will be women. There are plenty of 'jobs for women'; indeed, the numbers of both full and part-time positions for women have grown steadily since the early 1980s, while full-time jobs for men have continued to decline.

Between 1967 and 1987, the number of men in employment excluding the armed forces and government training schemes dropped from 15,896,000 to 13,951,000 with major job losses in full-time employment in heavy industry. At the same time, the number of women in employment, again excluding the armed forces and government training schemes, rose from 8,672,000 to 10,629,000. In the 15 years between 1972 and 1987, the pattern of work for both women and men changed dramatically, as shown in Tables 1.5 and 1.6.

Table 1.5: *Male employment in thousands*

Year	Type of employment		
	Full-time	Part-time	Self-employed
1972	13,011	620	1604
1987	10,866	908	2178
Difference between years	−2145	+288	+574

Table 1.6 *Female employment in thousands*

Year	Type of employment		
	Full-time	Part-time	Self-employed
1972	5587	2914	398
1987	5712	4254	713
Difference between years	+125	+1340	+315

Source (both tables): Employment Gazette Statistics, November 1989

The trend is expected to continue. By 1995, according to the Department of Employment, four in five new jobs will be taken by women. Politicians and employers alike have seen the practical implications of these figures and spelled out or introduced measures to help women re-enter work and to combine employment with domestic responsibilities. But many people are still far from coming to terms with the psychological impact of so many women having serious working careers.

■ The challenge of unisex work

For some women the greatest shock has been to find themselves the bread-winners, not only for themselves but also for their families. Their former state of financial dependency may have been irksome but was safe and familiar. Losing it has demanded personal adjustment, often along with major adjustment for their domestic partner. Not least of the problems has been to find a new basis for mutual respect.

At work, advancement may have brought further role conflict; perhaps leaving segregated 'women's work' behind and the need to face others' and their own doubts about combining femininity with effective management. Sources of 'help' in this area range from training courses on managerial skills to womens' magazines' guidance on the dress and behaviour required in the new situation.

But at least this role change has brought the benefits of a better income and the self-respect derived from having useful talents recognised. Many men simply feel under threat. Challenges for good jobs have increased and are now coming from the sex which was once expected to play an obedient and subordinate role in the workplace. Ways of behaving towards women which were more or less acceptable, or at least accepted in the traditional situation, are clearly inappropriate when the woman is your colleague or boss; indeed, they may be strongly resented. How many a middle-aged executive has treated a young woman colleague with the warm hearted, avuncular courtliness he uses when addressing his nieces, only to learn that he has provoked furious irritation? New relationships have to be established which are clearly distinct from the private relationships established with women as mothers, wives, sisters, daughters or lovers, and failure to establish them carries penalties for the individual and the organisation and for work harmony.

These challenges at work may be reinforced by challenge at home, when a spouse resumes her career or becomes increasingly successful at work. Although a growing number of men are beginning to accept this new situation and even find its compensations (being the sole breadwinner and fierce male competition had their drawbacks) it is not surprising that women on the way up have met with a good deal of discrimination, hostility and harassment.

Perhaps some such influences have been at work in the tardy implementation of equal pay. Indeed, the UK government's response to the European Commission's Directive to amend our equal pay laws has been so cynical as to raise the suspicion of spitefulness. Between 1975, when the Equal Pay Act was introduced, and 1989, women's weekly pay as a percentage of men's average weekly earnings has actually dropped from 73 per cent to 63 per cent.

■ Women's work motivation

It has to be said that women have not always helped their supporters. For instance they have not always responded as expected to opportunities which their men colleagues would welcome. Various studies[3,4] have shown a dichotomy in the attitudes of working women towards their careers. In the UK the majority of women in employment or returning to work still give priority to domestic responsibilities. They may seek interesting work but will give preference to a good salary and working conditions compatible with family life. This group may exasperate employers (and other women) by accepting work well below their capacity and even by criticising women who do put their careers first.

Included in this latter group are women who have given up domestic partnerships and children in order to work. This gives their job an added importance for them and they expect it to provide interest and chances for personal development. Surveys suggest they may be less motivated by high salaries than their male colleagues but more impatient of boredom. Those with sought-after skills may see advancement, not in braving out discrimination in one organisation and eventually gaining promotion, but in moving from one company to another, working upwards in salary and responsibility each time. Many others have left to set up their own businesses.[5] The numbers who have done so appear in Table 1.6. Employers used to an exclusively male senior workforce are having to adapt to these different values.

■ Domestic life can no longer be left at home

The domestic strains experienced by men and women in adjusting to their new work and social roles are further discussed in Chapter 3. Here, it is sufficient to note one final major effect upon working life.

There was once a time when employers could ignore their staff's domestic problems and treat as unacceptable any impact such difficulties might have on work performance. Sir Robert Hyde, founder of the Industrial Society (then the Industrial Welfare Society) used to tell the story of an employer at the turn of the century who prosecuted a man for trying to hang himself in the factory yard. At that time, suicide was a criminal act. The employer was unconcerned with the domestic circumstances which had driven the man to this state of despair. As late as the 1950s, a Midlands employer described how he had dealt with a case of persistent alcoholism by sending the man home in a van for his wife and small children to deal with.

This ability to ignore the other half of an employee's life has now disappeared and its disappearance is very largely due to the arrival of more women in more prominent and key positions in the workplace. It is simply not possible for most women nor for many men to pretend that domestic life has no impact on life at work, in the way many managements used to assume.

What is happening, therefore, is that major readjustments both at work and in private relationships have been required of very many employees, all within the working life of people still in their forties. Neither employees nor employers can afford to underestimate this revolution. It cannot be ignored and is a prime area where counselling to improve understanding and acceptance of change may help.

■ References

1. *Social Trends 19*, HMSO,1989.
2. *Young People and the Labour Market – A Challenge for the 1990s*, NEDO Training Commission, July 1988.
3. Bartos, R., *Marketing to women: a global perspective*, Heinemann Professional, 1989.
4. Lewis, S. and Cooper, C.L., *Career Couples*, Unwin Hyman, 1989 and Cooper, C.L. and Davidson, M., *Women in Management*, Heinemann,1987.
5. Herz, L., *The Business Amazons*, Andre Deutsch, 1986.
6. *Social Trends 19*, HMSO,1989.

2. New Jobs:
New Working Conditions

■ **Summary**

Changes in the structure of the working population have been matched by changes in types of jobs. Work in heavy manufacturing has declined drastically, while work in the service industries has developed. Work requiring use of modern technology has increased. Technology has permitted flexible hours of work and working from scattered locations. The changes have favoured women more than men and the qualified more than the unqualified. Sought-after employees have been accommodated with changes in working conditions in recognition of their domestic responsibilities. On the other hand, some work has required frequent relocation with great disruption to individuals and families. The pyramidical structures of the traditional organisation are being replaced by less rigid, less formalised structures with a greater variety of contractual arrangements between employer and employee.

These fluctuations in employment prospects and conditions, combined with changes in family life, have contributed to major changes in attitudes to employment. Many now expect much more of work than a pay packet; they look for interest and personal development in the service of an enterprise with values they can respect. They are asked to give much and they expect much in return.

Managing these independent people, who may be working at different times in different places within an increasingly amorphous organisation, requires very high levels of interpersonal skill. Individuals at all levels in these new organisations are likely to benefit from time to time from effective counselling.

While the working population has changed, jobs have been changing too, even more rapidly and with equally powerful implications for individuals and families. For a start, the jobs which disappeared in the seventies and early eighties did not simply reappear unaltered as the economy picked up in the late eighties. Many had disappeared for good, others were greatly changed and yet others were entirely new.

■ **The demands of the new jobs**

The permanent losses have occurred above all in the heavy manufacturing industry. These were the traditional areas for male employment, whether unskilled, semi-skilled or highly skilled. The loss of millions of jobs from manufacturing, mining and utilities is expected to continue, with a further 320,000 to go by 1995. Twenty-two thousand jobs disappeared in the last quarter of 1989 alone, exported overseas or rendered obsolete by the introduction of computers and robots. One large-scale clothing manufacturer in America now daily calculates the demand from a thousand retail outlets, transmits requirements to Hong Kong, Sri Lanka and Singapore and has a Boeing 747 deliver the new order within a week of ordering. And the whole transaction costs less that it would if produced more slowly and with greater risks of disruption (from labour, suppliers and transport) in his own factories.

Many men dispossessed by computers are not easily reconciled to a 'meaningless' rejection of their slowly acquired skills and years of commitment to work which carried status and value. As an angry Fleet Street printer put it:

You needed real men to get out the newspapers on the old system. You try setting the print and lifting the trays onto the presses all night every night – that's hard work and what's more, you've got to get it right first time. I took years to learn my job. Now they sit at these little desks and tap it out on a typewriter. There's nothing to it; anyone can learn it in six months. It's a silly job. A *girl* could do it.

■ Gender neutral: more brains

Silly or not, a girl *could* do it. The new jobs, by and large, require much less brawn than those which are gone. An automated factory can be run by half a dozen good technicians and still turn out double or treble previous production.

Job growth has been largely in computer-based industries and in the areas of employment where personal service is still required, with the largest increases in financial services, distribution and leisure. In the financial sector 141,000 new jobs were created in 1989 alone. But personal service characterises the job areas in which women have predominated. If not by nature, then by upbringing and tradition, they have been drawn to work which requires good relationships with others. Thus many job changes have favoured them, by reducing demand for physical strength exercised in physically demanding conditions and increasing demand for friendly, effective communication, understanding of customer needs, selling, negotiating and personal care.

Other changes have favoured the qualified of either sex. The eight years between 1979 and 1987 saw a 33 per cent increase in graduate jobs and a further 30 per cent growth in professional and managerial jobs is expected from 1987–95.[1] It takes brains to make good use of modern technology as well as to understand modern banking, hotel systems and transport. But brains are unisex as employers, some rather reluctantly, have come to accept. Over the four years 1983–7, employment participation rates for male graduates rose by 1.9 per cent, with a large increase in the employment of under 25 (from 78.9 per cent to 86.1 per cent). But employment for women graduates rose by 5.3 per cent overall (to 80.9 per cent) despite a drop of 3.6 per cent in employment for those aged 55-9.

These changes are reinforcing the challenge which is anyway presented by women's increasing work participation at skilled and managerial levels. Senior people, women as well as men, may find it even harder to respond to juniors with better qualifications than they have themselves, when those juniors turn out to be young women.

■ Adapting to family life

A further need for adjustment arises when this talented group marries and starts a family. Over the past two decades, women have increasingly delayed the birth of their first child, a tendency which has been most marked among the better qualified. They have chosen first to establish their careers and earning capacity, with the result that maternity may present an employer with the prospect of losing a valuable member of staff in whom the firm has made a large investment. One Personnel Director began to introduce career breaks and re-entry training in a hurry when one of the firm's section heads, a married women in her early thirties, announced that she was pregnant. Out of 28 section heads, he suddenly realised 17 were married childless women in their thirties.

The parental and domestic responsibilities of key staff have been increasingly allowed for in the form of part-time work, flexi hours, job sharing and parental leave and flexible retirement arrangements. More workplace creches are being provided and this facility is sure to increase, considering the fact that parents are given tax relief on their contribution to creche costs, following the 1990 Budget. Although Britain has not so far ratified the European Directive on parental leave or rights of part-time employees, the need to keep good staff has led many employers to anticipate these requirements or move ahead of them.

■ Home and location more flexible

Technology has not only brought more jobs to qualified people regardless of gender. It has also made easier the adjustments needed to accommodate staff with family responsibilities. Main frame computers need 24 hour attendance; they do not need large numbers of staff clocking on at 9.00 am and leaving at 5.00 pm. Desktop computers have reduced the need for work to be carried out at fixed hours in fixed locations. They have contributed to the rapid growth in part-time jobs, job sharing and flexi-time arrangements. They so much improve communication that many more people can choose where as well as when to work, for much of the week.

Working from home is no longer synonymous with sweated labour, with employees working long hours for cut price wages while the employer is relieved of the costs of accommodation and services. Now it can mean well-paid contract work, using a computer at times which fit in with domestic commitments, and avoiding the stress (and public pollution) of daily commuting. In 1969 when her request to go onto part-time work was turned down, Steve Shirley left her job and founded the FI Group to use qualified staff in just this way. The organisation now employs over 1,000 women, 75 per cent of whom are skilled computer programmers working from home. ICL now employs 400 home-based computer programmers (of whom 20 are men) and plans to increase the number. Professor Charles Handy of the London Business School has forecast that 20 per cent of the workforce will be home-based by the year 2000 AD.

Home-based workers may be out of sight but cannot be out of mind. Their work queries must be settled promptly, their equipment serviced, their needs for retraining met. Their manager may be the main person to relieve the isolation of home work and may need to develop more complex ways of keeping contact than were required when their office was down the corridor. Steve Shirley found a creative solution to this problem. She assigned all her home workers to monitoring teams so that, in addition to their own contract work, they have a responsibility to work on a team which monitors and assists progress on others' projects.

■ Smaller work teams

Meanwhile, in many offices, jobs have been cut but the importance of those remaining has increased. The staff still in posts are correspondingly highly skilled and versatile. If they perform below standard or leave the organisation the impact is that much greater and the difficulties of replacement that much harder. And, a factor which is often ignored or underestimated, managing such staff effectively can be highly demanding in terms of both time and communication skills.

In fact, office work forces are increasingly typified by small teams similar to those managed in modern production plants. For an example, read the case of Ted Bridges in his brewery (Chapter 6). His team is made up of highly skilled people with complementary skills, who have to work willingly together. Any problems they encounter need to be resolved quickly, probably in round table discussions. Anyone sent to manage them needs, like Ted, a democratic, consultative style and intense concern for the quality of communication within the team and between the team and the larger organisation.

■ Mobility and relocation

Staff relocation within the UK has recently seen a decline. Companies which used automatically to require staff to relocate in accordance with business needs have now modified their policy due to employee resistance.

There are various causes for this resistance. Increasingly partners in dual career families have had to take into account each other's work situation; increasingly the education of children has taken priority over career prospects, especially when a parent is confident of his/her ability to find alternative work without relocation. Many employees were affected by the great discrepancies in house prices between North and South which prevailed through most of the 1980s. In addition, an obligation to relocate has been seen as indirect discrimination against women employees in view of their heavier domestic responsibilities. The Equal Opportunities Commission has investigated a number of companies, including Marks and Spencer, on this score.

An additional factor has been the rising cost to employers of relocation, estimated in 1987 as involving up to £10,000 in direct costs and £20,000 additional expenses.The overall effect has been that by the mid-eighties the CBI estimated that only about 250,000 staff were moving annually at the employer's instigation. A survey on relocation of managerial and professional staff showed that only 40 per cent had relocated in the past decade and only 15 per cent had crossed the North-South border.[2]

This reduced movement may have contributed to family stability in some respects but has been offset in other ways. Nationwide mobility has been replaced by regional mobility, not requiring a house move but often greatly extending the length of time spent in commuting each day. This has imposed its own strains (see the Fig. 3.1 on page 20). And reduced relocation within the UK has not been matched by any similar reduction in relocation overseas.

Companies with overseas operations depend on key people undertaking frequent travel abroad or accepting residential assignments in another country. Of course, people have always travelled overseas in search of employment. But in the past they have predominantly been volunteers, responding willingly to opportunities for adventure and a freer life style. What is new is the increasing number of people who expected to remain in their home country, who are now being asked to spend months or years elsewhere.

The individual experiences culture shock and so may new colleagues in the host organisation. To the individual, daily life may bring strains; using a foreign language, coping with currency and different driving regulations, eating a different diet, learning customs which, even if unspoken, are still essential to acceptance. These difficulties must be tackled without the established support systems, the friends, possessions and small signs of status, which gave the individual a recognised identity and value back home. In this disturbing state, much that goes on in the new life may seem unattractive; normal behaviour may look hostile, different rules of hygiene seem disgusting, treatment of subordinates, animals, women and children may appear clearly uncivilised.

At the same time, the new hosts have problems. The newcomer lacks credibility. He (or worse still, she) cannot speak fluently, is far too young (or old), has the wrong skin colour, dresses inappropriately, treats people in funny ways and has some offensive mannerisms.

Although these feelings of alienation generally die down with time, the individual (and the hosts) may be faced with several such disturbances in a limited period and the most resilient may grow battle weary. Finally, there is the problem of re-integrating the returner back into the organisation's main-line career structure. The most brilliant employee, once out of sight, may fall out of mind. It is a poor reward for an overseas assignment to find some stay-at-home colleague has received the promotion you wanted for yourself.

■ Relocation and families

More problems arise if families are involved. A spouse must sacrifice an established home, community connections and perhaps an interesting career. She (or he) is not always prepared to give up these benefits to follow his/her mate around the world. While the job holder at least carries with him or her the familiarity of a work situation the other partner faces setting up a new home in a new environment often with little support. Children may have to be left behind or helped into new schools and new occupations and friendships. Not surprisingly, failure rates are high. One organisation has estimated that 50 per cent of failures in overseas placements are due to family unhappiness. The whole family may have to be returned to the UK or the marriage may break up. The emotional costs are great and so are the financial. One estimate puts the price of relocating a family at two and a half times the employee's base salary.[3]

■ Changing attitudes to employment

All these sorts of changes may have contributed to a growing independence of outlook in the working population and an assertion of personal values sometimes in opposition to the prevailing work culture. On the one hand, the many changes at work have shown the inadequacy of traditional values and standards as a protection for the individual. On the other, such changes have encouraged a broader perspective and more philosophical view of work as part of life experience.

Clearly, blind loyalty to an employer has no place in a world of mergers, buy outs, market collapse and skills obsolescence. It has not prevented massive redundancies of hitherto useful employees, often carried out with brutal haste.

Clearly, loyalty to the state has failed. The taxation which should have provided security in sickness and age and helped in family rearing has not provided any such thing and wealth is increasingly unevenly distributed through the population.

Clearly, getting a good training and working hard and honestly does not necessarily bring commensurate rewards in income, security and advancement while equally clearly, some half-way performances in privileged occupations are rewarded outrageously well.

The value of undertaking some types of work at all has also come into question. Not everyone feels happy to work in an armaments factory or an abattoir; but how about tropical forest clearance? Or tobacco manufacture? Or nuclear power? Or the production of drugs the safety of which has been challenged? Or work on buildings, roads and dams which involve the destruction of habitats?

The implications of these activities are now widely discussed in the media, and while some feel able to rebut criticism and some remain simply concerned to make sure the price is right, others are increasingly uneasy. The Personnel Director of a tobacco company recently admitted that work applications from graduates were steadily dropping and the inquiries had shown the company's product to be the major cause. A director of a large construction company commented on the increasing number of questions raised by staff regarding the environmental impact of their products and processes. In deciding on a job and how to carry it out a growing number of people are making up their own minds about what work is worthwhile pursuing. Growing numbers have been forced into greater self-reliance and a more precise assertion of personal values.

■ The new work values

The results of this process have been charted by organisations such as Taylor Nelson[4] and Applied Futures[5] which are employed in market research and by governments to identify long-term trends in personal values. From such studies it appears that increasing numbers in the working population will be concerned to seek work which permits personal growth and offers personal responsibility and autonomy. Surveys carried out in the UK in 1988 found these values being expressed by 38 per cent of the work population. A third remained interested in work primarily as a source of high earnings, status, position and power while a declining number (28 per cent) looked to a job simply for a secure weekly wage.

A very small new group was emerging of people who judged work experience in terms of the total range of experiences they might enjoy and total contribution they might make to community and environment. This group has moved far indeed from the predominent assumption of a few decades ago that work, whatever was available, would simply fill the decades and supply a living between school leaving and retirement.

Applied Futures suggests that tomorrow's European – the young people coming into employment – will increasingly be characterised by:

- Concern for the environment.
- Concern for self-development (mental, physical and emotional).
- Acceptance of individual responsibility.
- Enjoyment of complexity and ambiguity.
- Informality: rejection of conformity.
- Egalitarianism.
- Kinship with those of like interest, cross-nationally.
- Acceptance of regulations for collective efficiency, rather than order giving.

■ Changing organisations

As regards the organisations, here too change is overwhelming. The moves are from simple hierarchies to complex lateral and vertical networks; from concentrated to shared power; from status deriving from rank, to status accorded to expertise; from privileged protected information to information openly accessed; from (slow) adaptation to change to change initiation; from plans and targets to visions and intents; from the skills of organising and controlling to the skills of negotiating, persuading and making rewarding contracts.

Tom Peters, the American management guru, foresees concern for the individual customer as the key to 1990s success and the flexibility this will demand must shake all established hierarchy and bureaucracy.[6] The only management organisation chart worth heeding, he says, will be a plain circle with all the firm's employees inside and as few management ranks and job descriptions as possible. His vision has been part-way realised by many companies already. They form and reform ad hoc project teams to solve different problems, drawing together people from different departments or over world-wide locations. They form joint teams with customers, suppliers and government departments, or may second staff to outside organisations for long periods, to resolve mutual difficulties.

The image of a monolithic pyramid once used to depict company structure is fading rapidly; more and more appropriate is a cell-like image, continually pulsating, growing and shrinking as contract staff and teams are taken on or projects are completed and infant cells are acquired or hived off.

■ More complex management tasks

The leader's task, said the late, great Chester Barnard,[7] is to develop a network of co-operative relationships among all the people who have something to contribute to an economic enterprise. But in present circumstances, this task is increasingly complex. The leader must guide and motivate staff who may well be technically more highly qualified than he or she is, whose expertise is nevertheless crucial to decision-making. The leader must ensure fair and appropriate rewards when there are no obvious career paths and no appropriate promotion patterns and even money may prove a limited incentive. The leader may not share the values of either boss or subordinates or alternatively may feel strong sympathy with one and not the other. Some leaders may even wonder exactly who they do supervise. If a member of your team has been on secondment or has worked abroad independently for most of the year, in what sense are you able to assess their contribution and help to draw them effectively into a co-operative network?

Finally, today's leaders are finding that not all change is external. Their own values may be altering along with those all around them. In such circumstances, great demands are made on both the interpersonal skills and the equilibrium of individuals at all levels in the organisation. A counselling service can provide them with appropriate support.

■ References

1. Pearson, R. and Pike, G., *The Graduate Market in the 1990s,* Institute of Manpower Studies No. 167, 1989.
2. Syrett, M., Why staff say no to the big move, *Sunday Times,* 18 October 1987.
3. Piet-Pelon, N. and Hornby, B., *Women Overseas,* Institute of Personnel Management, 1989.
4. Taylor Nelson Research Limited, 44-6 Upper High Street, Epsom, Surrey KT17 4QS.
5. Applied Futures, 83-9 Kingsway, London WC2B 6SD.
6. Peters, T., *A Passion for Excellence,* Collins, 1986.
7. Barnard, C., *Functions of the Executive,* Harvard University Press, 1951.

3· Sources of Stress: the Work Environment

■ Summary

The major social changes outlined in the previous chapters have brought benefits to some, disadvantages to others and changes in work and family life to practically all. But all change, even beneficial change, involves adjustment. Some jobs require constant adjustment and some require continuing adaptation to difficult conditions. They are potent sources of stress. Aspects of working life which are known to provoke stress include adverse working conditions, poorly defined jobs, difficult colleagues, responsibility for others. Modern challenges include sex roles and value conflicts. All sudden and major changes have high stress potential.

Counselling can help to prevent the impact of difficult working conditions resulting in individual stress.

■ The costs and benefits of change

We can seldom add up in advance the true costs and benefits of the changes we experience. When Holmes and Rahe[1] developed their scale of the 'stress value' of change, 'good' and 'bad' changes alike were included. Of the 43 life happenings on their list, marriage, supposedly a happy event, ranked seventh in terms of the stress it created. Marital reconciliation came ninth, pregnancy twelfth, outstanding personal achievement mid-way. Holidays and Christmas are not without stress; indeed, some might be surprised to find that they come near the foot of the list.

Several of the changes in the list occur if work changes; giving a top score of 100 to Death of Spouse, Holmes and Rahe still gave significant ratings to changes which would be associated with most changes of job.

Business readjustments	39
Change to different line of work	36
Change in responsibilities at work	29
Change in living conditions	25
Review of personal habits	23
Change in work hours or conditions	20
Change in residence	20
Change in social activities	18

The one certainty about change is that it cannot be achieved without some cost. The play (later film) *Shirley Valentine* was about a Liverpudlian housewife who managed to break away from the stereotyped role she had played for 20 years. Its message looked old fashioned in 1989 but there was a message, not least for feminists, in the difficulty Shirley experienced in altering her life. The home which Shirley ran was empty of all stimulus and of all affection; it contributed nothing to the lives of its inhabitants nor to the community around. It was kept going by fear of change, indeed by fear of looking for richer alternatives. Even so, Shirley's first step away from this desolate situation into a much more enjoyable life was small and cautious and taken very slowly with great trepidation.

Everyday life presents us all with some level of challenge. We may have to adapt in any one day to disrupted travel, changed timetables, unexpected visitors, the absence of key people, deadlines or new assignments. We may have to get through a day when nothing happens at all. For the most part these changes are within our capacity to cope; we may even enjoy some of them and find others irritating, but we do not become distressed. It is when these 'normal' changes escalate in magnitude or rapidity or occur all at once and our 'normal' ability to adjust proves inadequate, that we begin to experience stress.

■ The experience of stress

The stage at which our normal coping ceases to be effective differs for each one of us. At one end of the scale are the highly nervous, anxious types who have difficulty in coping with a quiet domestic life and may not be capable of holding down any sort of a job. At the other are the people capable of handling world scale responsibilities or stepping into a capsule to be fired off into outer space. Whatever their capacity for adjustment, once that capacity is overstretched by events the individual begins to suffer, mentally and physically. They begin to experience the symptoms of stress.

This chapter looks at elements in the work situation which are known to increase the risk that staff who experience them will succumb to stress. Awareness of these elements may enable an organisation to mitigate them (see Chapter 14) or prepare to offer help to individuals who show signs of finding them intolerable.

Western societies generally present a high and increasing level of challenge. Many would claim that this has become very noticeable in Britain over the past two decades. Some surveys indicate that an increasing percentage of the population can no longer cope with the level of challenge daily life presents. Loss of employment may begin the process which leads them to withdraw from social and family relationships and cease to struggle to maintain a home. Finally some abandon even the attempt to meet expected standards of behaviour, dress or hygiene and join the ranks of the unemployable.

These people drop out not only because their jobs have disappeared but because, for all the reasons outlined in the previous chapters, work has become more demanding. How stressful a job is to the individual of course depends heavily upon the individual's resilience and also upon how well they are suited to the work. Chapter 4 explores these issues.

■ Jobs which involve stress

The uniqueness of an individual's relationship to their job nevertheless has not prevented research from discovering that some jobs stress more people than others and that some elements in all work distress a high proportion of job holders. Many of these studies are summarised in Michael Argyle's *The Social Psychology of Work.*[2] Cary Cooper has undertaken a great deal of work in this field and his researches are well summarised in his book, *Living with Stress.*[3] His study of stress experienced in a range of occupations showed that on a nine-point scale, miners came highest at 8.3, followed by policemen at 7.7. Construction workers, journalists and civil pilots came next at 7.5. Least stressful occupations were museum work (2.8) and library work (2.0).[4]

Cooper has also found high levels of stress among British managers and administrators. His survey of IBM managers and managers attending Henley Management College showed that in both groups a larger percentage claimed that their major stress was in the workplace than claimed it was at home, reversing the orders of magnitude established in Rahe and Holmes' international comparisons.

The sorts of stress that British managers particularly experience were indicated in Cooper's comparative study of over 1000 executives in ten countries. Figure 3.1 shows the factors mentioned by over 25 per cent of executives in Britain, Sweden, Germany and Japan. While all experience time pressure and work overload, Britons and Germans are particularly stressed by these factors and Britons alone in this group experience considerable stress due to the amount of travel their work requires.[5]

■ Common sources of stress at work

Some well defined sources of stress in work are:

1. Stressful working conditions.
2. Poor job descriptions.
3. Stressful relationships.
4. Changing sex roles.
5. Responsibility for other people.
6. Value conflicts.

Stressful working conditions

Physical conditions which contribute to stress at work have been extensively studied. It is not surprising that working in excessive heat or cold; in a distractingly noisy environment; in rooms which lack fresh air or good ventilation and in rooms lit only by artificial light, perhaps of a harsh glaring kind, all contribute to tension and discomfort. Some working hours are particularly stressful. There is evidence that working more than 40 hours a week reduces output. While all shift work disturbs sleep patterns and family and social life, maximum stress is produced by working rotating shifts which give no opportunity to adjust to these changes.

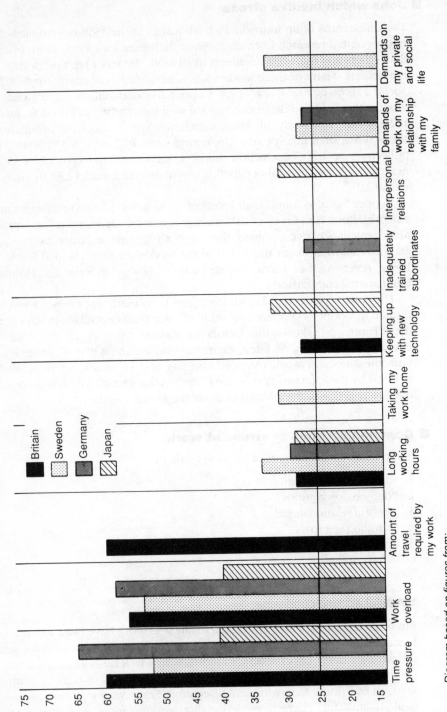

Diagram based on figures from:
Cary Cooper Executive Stress: a ten country comparison. Human Resource Management, 1984.)

Modern working conditions have reduced some of the discomforts of the past but have brought some special disadvantages of their own:

1. *Long working hours and excessive travel* (see Fig. 3.1). To actual working hours must be added the long periods which may be spent commuting each day. Not only does commuting ensure that large parts of each day are spent in non-productive work but it also carries with it the strain of dealing with traffic jams and train delays.
2. *The 'sick building syndrome'.* Office workers working in modern artificially ventilated offices often complain of headaches, stuffy nose and lethargy. The illness may have something to do with the lack of variety in the environment and loss of ability to control their surroundings. Any environment imposed upon us by others can increase the sensation of being treated like a battery hen required only for the eggs one can lay.
3. *Inability to control one's own work.* While much routine work has vanished from factories thanks to modern technology, some new strains have appeared in office work. A recent study showed that VDU operators find their work stressful because of its monotony, lack of control, constant pressure, breakdowns and physical strain. Lack of autonomy is an established cause of anxiety, depression and general mental ill-health.[6]
4. *Interruptions.* Many people are subject to the combined strains of working under pressure over long periods of time and being subject to constant interruptions, for example by telephone calls and visitors.
5. *Poor adaptation of premises* to current work needs and conditions. If the materials and equipment required for carrying out the work are arranged with little concern for workflow; if it is difficult to communicate with colleagues whose work relates to one's own; if the workplace is excessively cramped or spread out or if it imposes unnecessary isolation on the individual then the people concerned experience more or less strain and tension. The open plan office has not solved all communication problems; helpful for some operations, it has proved quite inappropriate to others. When accommodation is limited or only a few offices have windows, competition may exacerbate relationships between people who are ostensibly equal colleagues.

Poor job descriptions

It is still not unusual to find people at all levels in the organisation who do not have a written job description. There is potential for much misunderstanding, waste of effort, sense of unfairness and general anxiety where the job holder is left uncertain about their work objectives and responsibilities. There may be differences with a boss and with colleagues over the tasks to be done, the extent of responsibility to be exercised and the resources required to carry out a task effectively. Interference from above may seem excessive or alternatively a superior's support seem quite insufficient. Discrepancies between responsibility and authority can seriously reduce the job holder's capacity to carry out the job.

What about the case of someone with responsibility for negotiating on behalf of their organisation who is denied the authority to make a final decision? They know that this constraint seriously weakens this negotiating power, and so does the other negotiator. Other difficulties include tasks which make conflicting demands in terms of time or function; too few tasks or, more often, unrealistically many.

In addition to ambiguous or conflicting tasks, some jobs now involve role confusion or overload, with too many types of role to play in the course of the working day. Not every woman finds it easy to switch from managerial and professional responsibilities at work to nurturing and physical chores when she returns home to the family. Juniors may find that they are expected to behave as juniors in the office but to go out and act with great authority when dealing with clients on behalf of their organisations. Some people have great difficulty in managing the high standards of courtesy and informality which characterise much of modern management while remaining clear that this interaction is not to be confused with personal friendship. Various studies have shown that such role conflicts and ambiguities correlate with anxiety, depression, irritation and psychosomatic complaints.[7]

Of course, a written job description does not remove all conflicts within a job. Conflicting demands within the job are almost a characteristic of jobs in small organisations. But a written job description does mean that any discrepancies are openly recognised and can be accepted, discussed and regularly amended. Performance can be assessed realistically and failures not simply attributed to individual inadequacy.

Stressful relationships

It hardly needs stating that much stress arises from working with difficult colleagues, bosses and subordinates.

Bad bosses

Much stress is caused by those bosses who dodge their leadership and managerial functions or who use inappropriate management styles. Great difficulties arise in working for a boss who does not plan; who dodges making decisions; who does not treat people fairly; who is unduly friendly or remote; or whose management style is incompatible either with the work to be carried out or with the expectations of staff. Autocratic, democratic and bureaucratic leadership styles all have their place in the right circumstances but in inappropriate situations they spell disaster. No new ideas and solutions are generated by autocratic leaders. No urgent crises are resolved by democratic discussion. Bureaucratic leaders perform a valuable role in organisations where the main responsibility is to administer fairly the agreed rules for the community (for example, in some departments in the Civil Service), but wreck the organisation seeking to develop and adapt quickly to changing circumstances.

One style of leadership does appear to be universally destructive. It has been called ideocratic and relies on the appeal of the individual leader ('do it for my sake'). Outside management, it may be used by messianic crowd leaders. In management, it appears as a technique of the unskilled and inexperienced, as a weapon of last resort. It may tide a situation over but because it is a false appeal its ultimate effect is destructive and disaffecting.

If bosses can generate much stress, being a boss can be highly stressful. Responsibility for technical matters may pose difficulties but real stress comes with the responsibility for others. It is the leader who must sustain relationships for the sake of the whole, must cope with pressures from above and below and also from outside the organisation, must deal with frictions, accept blame for subordinates' limitations, confront outsiders on behalf of the department, confront subordinates where necessary and who has to attend, much more than any subordinate, demanding and seemingly unproductive meetings at work or in a social capacity. Jobs found to carry the highest levels of stress all involve responsibility for the safety and well-being of others (miners, policemen, construction workers, doctors, dentists and managers).

Tiresome colleagues

All the difficulties of dealing with bosses may be found, of course, in relationships with colleagues. Abrasive colleagues are wearing and colleagues who are too friendly take too much time. Highly competitive colleagues can add to fatigue because of the need constantly to treat them warily. Many committees are wrecked by the ego trips of inventive or self-promoting people or rendered intolerable by the domination of those who dislike challenge or of those who constantly question, analyse and restrain any new proposal.

Somewhere in the shift from middle to senior management a divide opens up between those who become aware that their new environment demands political as well as technical skills, and those who remain unaware or notice and decide such games are incompatible with their own personal values. Those who play politics may be irritated by their naïve or disapproving colleagues. Those who do not play note the politicians' ability to publicise themselves, denigrate others, flatter senior people and ingratiate themselves with the power groups in the organisation. They feel distressed when these tactics pay off and frustrated and let down that their own, technically equally competent, work does not result in their receiving equal recognition.

New technology may well exacerbate the problem of dealing with difficult bosses and colleagues because it results in a redistribution of power through the working group. An experiment with monkeys normally organised in male dominated hierarchies is illuminating. It took the form of continually changing the animals' social groupings so that they continually needed to re-establish the hierarchy of dominance.[8] This soon resulted in signs of stress and increased coronary artery disease. It is doubtful if such experiments could consciously be undertaken with human beings, but they are carried out all the time as a side-effect of other changes and can clearly provoke great anxiety.

Changing sex roles

The shift in the proportions of women in employment and of women in managerial positions has certainly highlighted the difficulty of redefining sex roles in the work environment. More and more men and women are having to adjust to working with the opposite sex in new posts as subordinates, colleagues and bosses. Women must adjust to the challenge of seeing other women playing roles they had assumed unattainable. Men must adjust to different roles in the home and in the family. The dual career family appeals to many couples but imposes strains of competition, exhaustion and childcare and leaves no free time for rest or relaxations. Both men and women are having to review and revise their traditional ways of dealing with personal needs for both independence and dependence. The many adjustments demanded of the individual in these circumstances are further considered in Chapter 4.

Responsibility for other people

Effective supervision of others demands a great range of skills depending upon many factors such as the size of the workforce, the tasks they have to perform, the levels of skill they must exercise, the degree of responsibility which they and the boss must carry for morale, health and safety, team and individual earnings and the constraints of time and resources within which the work must be completed.

While promotion to a supervisory post generally goes to the one who has shown most aptitude for and interest in advancement, this does not guarantee that the individual is automatically possessed of all the human relations skills the new job requires. Unfortunately, induction training into management posts is far from universal and the new managers and their teams may suffer while they acquire (or fail to acquire) needed skills. Yet more unfortunately, the tradition of rewarding a good employee with promotion is still powerful, even when this means taking a skilled person away from a job they do well to work in a post for which they have no aptitude. This happens particularly in work with a strong technical or scientific element, turning a good technician into an unhappy boss who damages work relationships for others and eventually loses his or her own self-esteem.

A modern problem is that of the manager who has worked competently in a post requiring a traditional role of task organisation and maintenance of staff morale but cannot manage the increasing pressures imposed by new competition and technology. She/he may have experienced rapid increases in demands for productivity and improved quality, changed and increased legal obligations and much greater pressure to meet deadlines. New technology may have posed technical challenges and threats to personal competence and may also have brought great staff changes. A new small team of highly trained employees may have replaced the group she/he knew well and may be expecting to discuss and negotiate where giving orders, delegating and training were once required. Yet these new democratic skills still need to be exercised with the objectivity and friendly impersonality which management demands.

Value conflicts

Successful organisations tend to develop a prevailing culture and on the whole to attract and retain people who share those values. One method of categorising organisational culture suggests what organisational values might attract which sort of individual.

Table 3.1 *Motivation and organisational culture*

Main motivation in work	In an organisation would lead to pursuit of:	In an individual would lead to pursuit of:
Realistic	Financial profit	High earnings
Investigative	Information; academic status	Research tasks and interests
Artistic	New expressions; cultural excellence public acclaim	Opportunities for artistic expression
Social	Enhancement of social/ leisure activities. Response to social need	Company of others, opportunities to help or to impress others
Enterprising	Development, innovation. Concern for growth	Opportunities to innovate, start something new,
Conventional	Safeguarding established ways. Maintaining and administering rules. Protecting tradition.	Work preserving traditions, administering routines, maintaining regulations.

Many companies now explicitly try to define their organisational culture and publish mission statements, for the benefit of staff, and recruitment brochures to attract new staff, which emphasise the values the company aims to uphold. In graduate recruitment, changes in statements of values as expressed in the recruitment brochure have been found noticeably to change the type of candidate who chooses to apply for employment with the organisation.

Certainly mutual dissatisfaction rapidly develops if those values are not clearly understood at the time of appointment. Selectors sometimes resort to mysterious statements such as, 'He's exactly our sort of person,' or, 'I simply can't see her ever fitting in.' Insofar as these comments go beyond personal prejudice, they may well imply a recognition that the individual's values do or do not seem compatible with those of the organisation.

This process of recruiting in one's own value image breaks down from time to time and may then be the cause of great distress. The company may deliberately try to break the mould. A dynamic tyro may be brought in specifically to smash old shibboleths and axe upholders of the old faith. Or a newcomer to a key post may inadvertently bring with him or her, along with the new knowledge and techniques for which they were appointed, alien ideas about work relationships or ways of dealing with customers and suppliers or attitudes towards established procedures. It is easy to see what major adjustments would be required if, in terms of the chart above, an individual seeking artistic outlets were by misadventure to join an enterprise devoted to profit-making or the protection of tradition. In such circumstances a power struggle develops which can only be resolved by modification on one side or the other or by a parting.

Changing attitudes towards employment were discussed in Chapter 2. There is some evidence that these attitudes are changing throughout the West and that the most radically different attitudes are held predominantly by the young. Thus it may happen that a company is led by senior people who assume that staff are motivated by high earnings, advancement and prospects of better status but finds it has recruited young people who assess their work situation in terms of its enrichment of their total life experiences. Some painful and costly selection casualties can be attributed to a mutual realisation of differences in values of this kind.

Finally there may be major conflicts of loyalties between groups in the same organisation or even between members of the same discipline. Auditors must, on occasion, come to terms with their own professional consciences when auditing some clients' financial data. Surgeons must face ethical decisions regarding the desirability or morality of some operations they are asked to perform. On hospital wards, decisions regarding the running of the ward can conflict with the nursing needs of particular patients. How do employees of an organisation ostensibly committed to environmental protection deal with the knowledge that some section of the business is using environmentally damaging processes or maintaining procedures which carry high environmental risk? The pain of resolving these dilemmas can only be partly eased by reference to the law or professional codes of conduct. In the United States, in particular, ethical issues have become recognised sources of conflict and are the subject of much discussion.

■ Sudden change

Finally, it is important to recognise the enormous potential for stress involved in any sudden change at work. Too often, organisations respond to market or financial information by rapid introduction of major changes. However desirable, the human cost is likely to be considerable.

Stressful change is characterised by:

1. Being unpredictable and unfamiliar.
2. Being involuntarily imposed.
3. Demanding a high degree of change.
4. Demanding very rapid change.
5. Providing the individual with no feedback on whether or not attempts to cope with events are succeeding.
6. Occurring in a situation where the individual lacks warmth and support from colleagues.

The process of adjustment which everyone must undergo in coping with such circumstances is too often damaged by evasions and platitudes ('You'll soon get over it,' 'You want to get yourself out of it,') or by putting off discussion ('I'll see you about it next week.'). Some managers escape from others by pulling rank ('Sorry, but I really am pressed. The show must go on. Personnel will see you.'). Others offer palliatives which may or may not alleviate but which amount to evasion ('Take the afternoon off.').

Much more helpful are the constructive responses characterised by counselling. The individual can be helped towards acceptance of any change if the news is confirmed by a trusted person; if someone is prepared to listen to their reactions; if they are helped to work out constructive ways of handling the new situation.

Counselling in management is not solely or mainly for helping people who are suffering from excessive stress. Its main contribution is to help in understanding behaviours, responses and actions which are not producing the results the individual needs. It is, however, a valuable technique in helping someone who is evincing early warning of stress and by the same token it can help identify what strains the organisation is imposing and what action might effectively reduce them.

■ References

1. Holmes, T.H. and Rahe, R.H., 'Rahe's Social Readjustment Scale,' *Journal of Psychosomatic Research*, **11**, 1967.
2. Argyle, M., *The Social Psychology of Work*, Penguin, 1989.
3. Cooper, C.L., Cooper R.D. and Eakin, L.H., *Living with Stress*, Penguin, 1988.
4. Cooper, C.L., 'Your Place in the Stress League', *Sunday Times*, 24 February 1985.
5. Cooper, C.L., 'Executive Stress: A Ten Country Comparison', *Human Resource Management*, 1984.
6. Caplan, R.D., Cobb, S., French, J.R.P., Van Harrison, R. and Pinneau, S.R., *Job Demands and Worker Health*, Institute for Social Research, University of Michigan, 1975.
7. Mackay, C. and Cooper, C.L., 'Occupational stress and health: some current issues,' in Cooper, C.L. and Robertson, I.T. (Eds), *International Review of Industrial and Organisational Psychology*, Wiley, 1987.
8. Manuck, S.B., Kaplan, J.R. and Matthews, K.A., 'Behavioural antecedents of coronary heart disease and atherosclerosis.' *Arteriosclerosis*, **6**, 1986.

4· Sources of Stress: Individual Response

■ Summary

When challenge turns into a source of stress the individual experiences physical and psychological change, which can lead on to illness. Modern ways of living make it probable that all of us will go through periods of stress in the course of a lifetime: adolescence, middle life and retirement each bring special sources of stress. To them must be added the stresses of unemployment or of living with the unemployed; the personal stresses at work of being in the wrong job and, especially for women, the problem of combining the responsibilities of work and home and facing up to the stresses which promotion can bring. Victims of stress at work reveal their state by changed behaviours which characterise low morale. Once this happens, the organisation may suffer damage as well as the individuals concerned.

■ When challenge becomes stress

Once life's daily challenges become excessive, and move beyond the individual's normal ability to cope, anxiety begins to climb. The reaction is both physical and psychological and may be measured both physically and psychologically. It can be assessed in terms of subjective tension such as feelings of dissatisfaction and a continuing sense of workload; by physiological measures of blood pressure, cholesterol, heart rate and adrenaline excretion; by incidence of heart attacks, ulcers and other stress-related illnesses; by changes in health related behaviour such as smoking and drinking. It can be measured by replies to the General Health Questionnaire (GHQ) developed by Goldberg which measures levels of anxiety, depression and the loss of all concern for others which has been described as burn-out.[1]

The process which results in such adverse reactions is well understood. Any external event which we perceive as a threat to our well-being results in the automatic activation of the pituitary and adrenal glands. The sympathetic nervous system takes over, heart rate increases, extra oxygen is delivered to the muscles and the body prepares itself generally either to fight off the danger or to flee it. As many an expert on stress has pointed out, this readying the body for 'fight or flight' was essential to survival in the days when the main dangers people faced were attack by man or beast, or the need to escape other physical danger. But neither fight nor flight is appropriate for dealing with modern mammoths such as a production deadline, making an important speech or going to an interview with a difficult boss.[2]

Any reaction beyond the heightened awareness required to put up a good performance must be kept under control.

■ Physical signs of stress

If alarming events are frequent, so that the individual is often and powerfully prepared for fight or flight and must often exercise severe self-control, then they may begin to develop physical reactions. They may develop muscular pain, typically in the neck, shoulders and back. They may suffer tension headaches. An excessively active digestive system may give rise to stomach pains and spasms and eventually to ulcers.

Stress can contribute to or trigger off a raft of illnesses: high blood pressure, heart disease, chronic back ache, bronchial asthma, dermatitis and eczema, diabetes, migraines, peptic ulcers and alcohol or drug dependence. Moreover, people under stress often adopt health-damaging behaviours such as reducing sleep, smoking and drinking excessively and eating poorly balanced diets and so render themselves more susceptible to illness.

Coronary heart disease is a major and growing cause of mortality in Britain. Scotland and Northern Ireland now have the highest rates in the world. Coronary heart disease has been convincingly linked to raised blood pressure, raised blood cholesterol and cigarette smoking. Any one of these three involves risk; two factors double the risk and three multiply the risk eightfold.[3]

All three factors are stress related. Most clearly established is the link between stressful experiences and increased blood pressure, but there are also indications that stress may raise blood cholesterol, while it certainly provokes many people into starting or increasing smoking. The anger and hostility which result from stress also increase the risk of coronary heart disease, more especially if the anger is suppressed.

■ Psychological signs of stress

Long before illness is established, however, the individual under stress will experience psychological reactions. They may become aware of increased irritability with others. They may become afflicted with indecision if too many important matters suddenly have to be decided in a hurry. Under prolonged strain they may begin to wonder if anything is worthwhile. Boredom and depression increase and so does general dislike of other people. Social skills deteriorate; responses become clumsier and more offensive; the will to communicate with anyone at all is weakened.

A sense of stress easily translates into a feeling of being persecuted and inability to cope. The individual may suffer feelings of futility and failure and may lose their sense of personal worth. 'Burn-out', typified by emotional exhaustion and inability to respond to others as human beings (depersonalisation) or to carry out work at a normal standard, is a particular form of stress which appears to be produced by dealing with very difficult people. While burn-out has been found to occur particularly in medical professions it is also found among administrators, supervisors and managers.

Whatever our level of resilience, we all share a need for equilibrium, a need to make sense of our experiences, to have some understanding of events, some control of them and some control of the feelings they provoke. We all want to establish and maintain some relationships and be able to relate to others in ways that express our intentions towards them. We all seek out the environments which enable us to do this most effectively and present us with no more than the challenges we can cope with.

Our tolerance of challenging circumstances appears to be unrelated to other attributes. Good intellectual ability may help in devising coping mechanisms but can also be used to exacerbate fears and anticipate fearful situations. Powerful emotions may produce the vigour and optimism to overcome difficulties but can also lead to undue despair. A more phlegmatic temperament may tide the individual over minor difficulties but be changed into ineffective passivity and withdrawal if life becomes overwhelming. Thus it comes about that the same life experiences may distress the nervous enormously but be readily accepted by others. All the same, it does seem that modern life is increasing the number of challenges and potential sources of stress that everyone must tackle.

■ Socially imposed stress

The lifestyles of the Western world ensure that certain periods of life are, for most of us, more stressful than others. Early upbringing imprints upon us ways of relating to others which will powerfully affect our future. It is also likely that we will face particular challenges in adolescence, mid-life and on retirement.

1. Early upbringing

Most of us are brought up in small two generation families where, in early childhood, we are overwhelmingly subject to the training provided by just two adults (or possibly one). The perils of parental pressure to achieve are well documented; equally damaging may be pressures to beat or keep up with older brothers and sisters. Conflicts about life goals and how to evaluate one's achievements are easily produced by parents whose own goals are confused. How is one to achieve a high income while devoting oneself to good works? How is femininity or masculinity to be preserved in occupations which have been the preserve of the opposite sex?

If all parental training is a mixture of blessings, we still need parents around. If these important people are absent for long periods, we may lack the models for adult behaviour altogether. Lack of training in how to handle adult roles and responsibilities will more or less seriously handicap the individual in taking on adult responsibilities.

2. Adolescence

This is the time when the individual must complete their formal education and move into adult life. But educational demands are increasing, along with the appreciation that educational failure presages failure in work and earning capacity of lasting consequence. Getting a job is no longer a question of following a parent or taking an apprenticeship or picking up whatever is going at the local exchange. On the one hand, any appropriate local employment may have disappeared altogether. On the other, the variety of possible jobs may have increased, together with the difficulty of learning about them and knowing whether or not it is worth one's while to apply for them.

All these challenges, moreover, have to be met at a time when most young people are thinking of other things. As one Oxford don put it: 'Very few of our students fail because they lack the necessary number of neurones. Most of them fail because they cannot manage the conflicting demands of sex, study and dirty socks.'

3. Mid-life crisis

The mid-life crisis is by now well documented. Traditionally this is the time when women face the menopause, the emptying nest and the adjustments required to go back into employment. They are not helped by a culture which equates (female) youth with desirability or by lingering mythologies about the crippling mental and physical effects of the 'change of life' or by employers' persisting discrimination against older people.

Men also experience or fear biological changes and may find daunting the prospect of continuing in current employment with increasingly reduced chances of advancement. Their major family responsibilities may be over and many adjustments will be required in domestic life. It may now become apparent that the reduced family is living in the wrong home in the wrong location and that its members have few interests in common. The future may not look enticing. Our population may be ageing but we do not revere age the more. We remain a society which assumes that from middle age onward the road is going to be downhill.

4. Retirement

Entry into retirement makes up the fourth phase of life in a Western society which can pose special challenges. Very few of us are now faced with destitution when we leave work and many of us retain some useful working relationship even after officially leaving. Nevertheless, it is a time when most people find their income is markedly reduced, when they must adjust their standards of living and manage without many small sources of status. Daily life has to be based at home instead of in various and varied locations and everyone in the home has to adjust accordingly.

These periods of especial challenge are not, of course, inevitable. They derive from the pattern of working and domestic life which living in an industrialised society has imposed upon us. Some are sure to be modified as patterns of working life are modified. But as things are, these are periods when people who are normally well able to cope may develop the symptoms of stress.

■ The major stress of unemployment

One source of stress which has greatly increased in Britain over recent decades is unemployment. It has to be said that, whatever the overall stresses of work,being employed appears to be much less stressful than being unemployed. A ten year study of British men who lost their jobs in 1971 found that their death rate over that period was 36 per cent greater than for the whole population of males aged between 15 and 64 and 21 per cent greater if age and class were equated. The figure for their wives was 20 per cent.[5]

Brenner has calculated that a one per cent increase in unemployment in the USA, if sustained for five years, would result in a 4.1 per cent increase in suicides, a 3.3 per cent increase in mental hospital first admissions, a 4 per cent increase in prison admissions, a 5.7 per cent increase in murders, a 1.9 per cent increase in deaths from alcoholism and 1.9 per cent in the total death rate.[6]

There are obvious practical reasons why unemployment should contribute to stress. The unemployed are generally poorer than the employed and poverty may result in poorer diet and clothing and fewer comforts and less warmth at home. Other behaviours which damage health seem related to stress; many unemployed acknowledge that they smoke and drink more, two behaviours which are detrimental to health.

Mentally the unemployed suffer the emotions of bereavement but may not recover well from the experience. The first reactions on becoming unemployed are generally ones of shock, anger and incomprehension. Many feel disorientated by the loss of an assured daily routine and programme of activities. These feelings are followed by fluctuations between optimism and pessimism as the individual looks for alternative work. If the search proves fruitless, the individual becomes increasingly apathetic. At last they may decide that their situation is hopeless and cease to look for work at all.[7]

Greatest distress is experienced, understandably, by those who are most attached to their jobs. They suffer more severely from reduced self-esteem and greater depression. In general middle aged men seem to suffer more than young people or married women.[8]

Other evidence that being in paid employment is less stressful than being unemployed comes from comparisons of the health of working women with housewives. Housewives may be fully occupied; but they may also be isolated, bored and frustrated. They go to see the doctor more often than those in employment and have more serious illness and lower life expectancy.[9] Overall the evidence is that women with jobs are better able to tolerate stressful life events and are in better mental health that their sisters who are full time at home. Involuntary unemployment is so extensive in Britain today that even those who are in employment are sure to know others who are not. To a greater or lesser extent they will be affected by the unemployed person's anxieties.

■ Stressful aspects of work

There remain plenty of stresses in work itself. Some work is particularly stressful for some types of people while some work appears to be stressful to a large number of people.

How stressful a particular job is to the individual, of course depends heavily on how well the individual is suited to that occupation. This is more than a matter of level of resilience. It relates to all aspects of temperament, ability and motivation. People who perform best when they are guided by rules, have a strong leader and know exactly what they have to do, suffer particularly if put into ambiguous or fluctuating conditions. Great stress can be caused to the individual put into a job which requires him/her to work at an 'unnatural' pace, whether faster or slower than they normally would.

The division into Type A and Type B personalities has proved a useful way of determining what kind of stresses each will be able to tolerate or will find intolerable. Type A personalities are workaholics, aggressively competitive and highly involved in their work. They have the feeling that everything is urgent and that time is short. Such people become extremely anxious if they have to work in a highly controlled environment where they have very little influence on events. Calmer Type Bs are much less worried by whether or not they are in control. On average, their careers do not progress as fast as those of their Type A colleagues. Nevertheless, quite a number of them get to the top of the tree; they have, after all, the supreme quality of survival.[10]

A job which superficially seems to suit an individual well may still contain elements which they cannot master and which are therefore high sources of stress. Those high on logic but low on creativity can impose great burdens upon themselves and others if they are in a job where new solutions are regularly required. Inability to sustain high levels of tension and vigilance may damage an otherwise useful performance. Jobs vary in the degree to which concern for quality and avoidance of any mishaps or faults is crucial; in the demands they make upon memory of different types of information; in the need to work meticulously in accordance with rules. Much stress can be generated if these sorts of requirements are not met by specific relevant abilities in the job holder. While good selection and promotion procedures can reduce these misfits, it remains important to continually review the content of jobs, to ensure that any misfit is kept as low as possible (see Chapter 14).

■ Combining work and home

The additional strains resulting from the increasing number of women in employment has been the subject of much study. A sensitive review of the issues is given in Judi Marshall's book, *Women Managers: Travellers in a Male World*.[11]

All women must juggle the responsibilities of work and home life, and those concerned to advance women make much of the continuing uneven distribution of domestic work and responsibilities. It seems obvious that when two adults are working equally hard outside the home they should agree to an equal division of the chores within it. But this common sense approach remains rare.

A 1987 survey[12] showed that, even where both partners work full time, in 72 per cent of households the woman still carries the main responsibility for running the house. In most homes it is women who continue to undertake the washing and ironing, cleaning and cooking and care of sick children. The tasks of shopping and dealing with household bills are more evenly divided but only in repairing household equipment do men generally take the main responsibility (82 per cent of households).

Attitudes are more liberal than actions, with never-married people more liberal than the married. Even among the never-marrieds, however, only 41 per cent consider the tasks of washing and ironing should be equally shared and only 55 per cent think cooking the evening meal should be a joint responsibility. Among married people, 27 per cent think laundry should be shared and 42 per cent think cooking. But when it comes down to actuality, only 9 per cent of couples shared the laundry and 17 per cent the cooking.

Women manage to combine the responsibilities of work and home by working shorter hours (and so earning less) and by reducing their leisure time. The majority of both women and men now accept a woman's right to go out to work and a significant proportion even consider she has an obligation to do so. But concomitant changes in the running of homes are slow to emerge.

This delay is, of course, partly caused by women themselves. While most protest, some still value their role as Queen of the Hearth and the best cook in town. Others may decide the habitual relationships they have established at home are worth more than the rows and disruption which a partner's re-education would involve. Yet others feel a need to highlight their domestic efforts to offset personal guilt and avert the domestic hostility which external success can bring.

A male partner's view of domestic sharing is also unlikely to be governed purely by logic and justice. Many chores are boring and the fact that his spouse is now having an interesting life outside the home does not seem to every man an obvious reason for taking over unattractive domestic work. Indeed, he may feel his spouse should demonstrate that her better life is not to his disadvantage. If he is coping with the competition of women colleagues at work, he may even exploit domestic dominance as a means of adjusting the balance and reducing the sense of threat he is experiencing.

These conflicts, both within oneself and with a partner, rumble on as a background to many working lives. They may amount to no more than irritation; they may flare up and become major sources of stress. But they are certainly difficult to resolve in ways which satisfy both partners and must be included in any understanding of the pressures of working life today.

■ Women and promotion

Much is heard of the 'glass ceiling' which prevents women from gaining the promotion their talents warrant and it certainly exists in many organisations. On the other hand, a complaint of some senior managers is that, far from being prejudiced against women, they have tried hard to advance promising women staff. Then, just when a talented protegé is reaching levels of major responsibility, she refuses promotion or resigns.

It is worth thinking why this happens. Perhaps some women tire of the rat race earlier than men. The reasons for continuing to sustain a heavy work-load, cope with major responsibilities and put up with much travelling and frequent relocation may begin to look increasingly inadequate. Is it worth working in such a way, simply in pursuit of promotion to more of the same? Many men in middle life ask such questions and women are aware that pro-motion carries some extra disadvantages for them.

One extra disadvantage will be increasing isolation because, as yet, few women are promoted to senior ranks. Being the only woman at this level, the female manager may well be excluded from gatherings, networks and interests traditionally designed exclusively for males. They may also lack the support which home life can bring, either because they live alone or be-cause they have a partner uninterested in their careers.[13]

Then, because of their rarity, senior women executives are highlighted and their performance tends always to be on trial. They cannot admit to weakness, even to the degree that a male colleague might be allowed. Talk-ing things over with male colleagues may not always be easy. Some prob-lems are difficult to discuss with the opposite sex, more especially if the opposite sex is the cause. As newcomers to the field they may have self doubts and are sure to lack role models. They may well be short on training in building teams, political skills and planning a career, the skills which are more emphasised in boys' upbringing than girls'.

There seems to be little difference between men and women in the way they react to similar stress at work. But women are subject to greater stress, and there is some evidence that they take longer to unwind after a stressful day.[14]

All in all, while all these challenges may fail to daunt some women, it is hardly surprising that they may still suffer considerably from stress. Nor is it surprising that others decide to settle for a less dramatic career.

■ Recognising stress

There are therefore many potential sources of stress in modern life and work. The individual concerned is the person who will first experience the mental or physical warnings. Nevertheless, these private warnings will soon be translated into behaviours which others can observe. A good timekeeper starts coming in late; someone who always meets deadlines begins to miss them; a constructive conciliatory member of the team becomes an irritable nit-picker who makes untypical attacks on others.

Behaviour at meetings changes. In a healthy meeting everyone contributes, problems are shared and members show a recognition of each other's values and a determination to resolve difficulties together. Meetings of people who are under stress are markedly different. Discussion is aggressive: some members attack while others withdraw into passivity. There is much scapegoating and disaffection and plenty of non-verbal behaviour indicating withdrawal, lack of interest and hostility. The behaviour of key people is crucial. Once they demonstrate disaffection, poor morale quickly runs through the group.

Epidemics of illnesses are linked to poor morale. Once it becomes expected that people will be ill, many succumb; they expect to be ill; they remember past illness; they remember stories that this type of building makes people feel ill; they tell each other how ill they feel. Similar moods stimulate absenteeism and lateness, complaints, grievances and sabotage.

A very low level of morale has been reached and many employees will be experiencing stress when these sorts of behaviours begin to escalate in an organisation. They cause individual suffering, are immensely wasteful of human ability and immensely costly. *The Economist* has claimed that up to ten times more weekdays lost to industry are due to stress than to strikes. A *Guardian* investigation produced the estimate that stress costs British industry, at a conservative estimate, £1.3 billion a year in increased alcoholism, absenteeism and premature death and retirement. Senior management at Xerox gave the cost of replacing one executive lost due to stress as around £400,000. These are alarming figures, well worth trying to reduce and avoid. Any enterprise must be concerned to introduce all the measures it can to offset such adverse results of change.

■ How counselling helps

Among the services an organisation could provide, counselling must come high. Definitions of counselling are legion, but through them all some themes persist. Counselling is seen as: 'the process ... of giving ... help'; 'a two-person situation in which one person ... is helped to adjust' and 'to resolve his/her problem(s)' so as to 'become a happier and more productive member of his society'. It is seen as a learning situation in which the counsellor enables someone to resolve conflicts, reduce anxieties and develop new and more appropriate responses. It does not need to be performed only by those who have received professional training as counsellors. It is, above all, a process of active listening, of giving the other 'an opportunity to explore, discover and clarify ways of living more satisfyingly and resourcefully,' a way of enabling a person in difficulties to weigh up their situation, become more aware of their own coping resources and their own needs and finally to make their own decisions as to how best to respond.

■ Is counselling a legitimate management function?

Does this recognition of the value of counselling in times of stress entirely resolve doubts about the relevance and legitimacy of counselling as a management function? Deeply rooted in the management tradition is the view that workers – not people – go to work. As workers, they are supposed to offer skill, commitment and obedience in a collaborative but impersonal relationship and receive in return wages, security and advancement. They are not supposed to bring their emotions to work; their private feelings, domestic worries and personal values are dealt with outside working hours. Workers are 'strong' and can be expected to handle worries and private feelings on their own. Emotional vulnerability is a disqualification for work, along with physical and mental frailty. Weak, sick, vulnerable people are not in employment. They should not be; they should be at home or looked after elsewhere in appropriate institutions.

Such an ethos is, of course, seriously challenged by the view that personal worries can (still more, should!) be tackled at work, particularly by the provision of any service as personal as counselling. Managers with this ethos may well see counselling at work as an unwarrantable, indeed impertinent, intrusion into individual privacy, and perhaps more seriously one which undermines the development of self-reliance and any sense of personal responsibility.

But our review of what is happening to work and to people's attitudes to work shows how much times have changed. Increasingly today it is the whole person who comes to work and it is the whole person who is needed at work. Many jobs cannot be performed by people who turn up simply to exercise their skills. To carry out their work effectively they must also exercise independent judgement and commit themselves to furthering the well being of the enterprise. They must do so to an extent which involves their whole personality and intrudes upon family and leisure life. Such involvement and commitment brings the corollary that the job holder is increasingly vulnerable to distress when working circumstances change or working relationships go sour. In these circumstances a counselling service designed to help the individual handle these experiences appears entirely proper and indeed one which employers might be expected to provide. The time may not be so far distant when a counselling service is accepted as routine in much the same way as health and safety regulations, training and monitoring are accepted now.

■ Is counselling just manipulation?

One more concern remains. By what right do employers manipulate the individual's feelings simply so that he or she will be able to handle the otherwise unacceptable strains their job demands?

It must be acknowledged that a good deal of training in appraisal interviewing has some flavour of this approach. The skills of listening are sometimes taught as though it were the appraiser's job to listen to the other so as to help them to come to adopt a constructive approach to any difficulties their work situation may present. Counselling does indeed carry the risk of becoming one-sided and manipulative. But a counselling service at work has two quite legitimate functions:

- It can properly be used to help the individual who needs help because some traumatic experience has temporarily robbed him or her of their normal capacity to deal with events.
- It can properly be used to help both sides to adjust to change.

The second function is a reminder that the manager who listens to his subordinates with the concentration and empathy good listening requires cannot fail to be changed in the process. He or she must gain an understanding of a situation in which they themselves are involved and to which they themselves must have contributed. The situation cannot be fully understood unless this contribution is included and assessed as objectively as possible.

Counselling of this order is the opposite of paternalism. It releases both counsellor and counsellee from the stereotypes of hierarchy and frees them both, in the words of the British Association for Counselling, 'to explore, discover and clarify ways of living more satisfyingly and resourcefully'. Both counsellor and counsellee can become more aware of their talents, limitations and needs and both can develop a better capacity to face crises and resolve them successfully.

This concept of counselling as an enabling process is entirely in tune with emerging thinking of the company as a learning organism. The company grows and recreates itself insofar as all its component members retain and develop creative powers and have the opportunity to express them.

Perhaps in future the company which most readily attracts the people it needs will be the one which sees its prime task as helping the individual to develop and harness his/her own resources in the service of the enterprise. It could expect to retain that individual for only as long as this development continued and would judge careers more in terms of the continuation of development than in the provision of steps up a job ladder. In such a scenario, counselling would become a key management skill.

■ References

1. Goldberg, D., *Manual of the General Health Questionnaire*, National Foundation for Educational Research, Windsor, 1978.
2. Arroba, T. and James, K., *Pressure at Work, a Survival Guide*, McGraw Hill, 1987.
3. Johnstone, D.W., 'Will stress management prevent coronary heart disease?' *The Psychologist*, July, 1989.
4. Maslach, C. and Jackson, S.E., 'Burn out in health professionals: a socio-psychological analysis,' in Sanders, G.S. and Saul, J. (Eds), '*Social Psychology of Health and Illness,*' Erlbaum, 1982.
5. Moser, K.A., Fox, A.J. and Jones, D.R., 'Unemployment and mortality in the OPCS longitudinal study', *Lancet Two.* 1324/9, 1984.
6. Brenner, M.H., *Estimating the Social Costs of the National Economic Policy: Implications for Mental and Physical Health and Criminal Aggression*, US Government Printing Office, Washington, 1976.
7. Kelvin, P. and Jarrett, J., *The Social and Psychological Effects of Unemployment*, Cambridge University Press, 1985.
8. Waugh, P.B., 'Work and Unemployment,' from Drenth, P.J.D. (Ed) *Handbook of Work and Organisational Psychology*, Wiley, 1984.

9. Hoare, H.A. 'Women, Work and Stress: A Review and Agenda for the Future', *Journal of Health and Social Behaviour*, **23132/44**, 1982
10. Chesney, M.A. and Rosenman, R., 'Type A Behaviour in a Work Setting,' in Cooper, C.L. and Payne, R. (Eds), *Current Concerns in Occupational Stress*, Wiley, 1980.
11. Marshall, J., *Women Managers: Travellers in a Male World*, Wiley, 1984.
12. *Social Trends*, HMSO 19, 1989.
13. Hartingdon Mills, S. and Stern, A., 'Should stress management be company policy?' *Women Into Management*, **4**, 1989.
14. Frankenhaeuser, M., Lundberg, U., Frederickson, M., Melin, B., Tuomisto, M. and Myrsten, A., 'Stress on and off the job as related to sex and occupational status in white collar workers,' *Journal of Organisational Behaviour*, **10**, 1989.

5· What Do We Mean by Counselling?

■ **Summary**

In this chapter, we look at some of the fundamental issues of counselling: what it is, and what it isn't. The skill of counselling is central to the activities of a manager. It is therefore crucial that every manager understands what counselling is, and when and how to use it.

Counselling in management means:

- Being non-directive.
- Being non-judgemental.
- Empathy.
- Confidentiality.
- Helping to release tension.
- Helping to release creative energy.
- The client wants it.
- Ownership of the problem stays with the 'client'.

Counselling in management does *not* mean:

- Sympathy.
- Advice.
- Giving or forcing solutions.
- A 'soft' option.
- Vagueness.

The skills of counselling are the skills of creating and maintaining good human relationships. As such, they are of prime importance to all managers.

Counselling is one of the most productive tools a manager can use. Why?

Because it involves recognising the importance of a member of staff by spending time listening to them. There is very little as motivating to the human race as the thought that someone is interested in them. We all need approval and seek it in varying ways. Giving recognition to staff by giving them time is the most powerful and least used motivator. It is *not* a soft option, and is a great deal more difficult than telling someone what to do and how to do it. That demands few skills, and has a very short term effect. It is unlikely to solve an underlying problem, and will not guarantee the recipient's commitment to the solution.

The purpose of counselling is *not to tell people what to do, but to help them explore and understand the situation they are in.* Only when they have done this can they deal with the situation.

If management is about developing staff to their full potential in order to work at their most productive for themselves and the organisation, then counselling is a crucial skill for the manager. **The skills of counselling are the skills of creating and maintaining good human relationships.** As such, they should be of prime importance to *any* manager.

Counselling is a much abused word. It can mean everything from a quick word in the corridor to a series of regular hour long sessions. In terms of counselling in the workplace, it will probably mean both of these and some other activities in between. It can be done to varying degrees by line management, functional managers, personnel staff, or external staff. The appropriate person will vary with the situation and client. Even if, as a manager, you never officially 'counsel' anyone, it is vital that you understand what it is, and what it can do. On reading about counselling, you may find you do a lot of it, but do not call it counselling. It is therefore important to understand what it is you have been trying to do, and whether you might improve on your methods. It is important to accept that counselling is not just something that social workers and therapists do, but an indispensable part of the manager's routine.

■ Defining counselling

Among all the definitions of counselling, some themes persist. Counselling is seen as:

'the process ... of giving ... help to persons suffering from fully conscious conflicts.'

'a two person situation in which one person ... is helped to adjust ... to himself and to his environment.'

'a face to face relationship in which ... [one person] ... is consciously attempting by verbal means to assist another person to modify emotional attitudes which are socially maladjusted.'

'a learning oriented process ... in which a counsellor ... seeks to assist [the other person] ... to learn more about himself ... [and to develop] ... more realistic ... goals [so] that [he] may become a happier and more productive member of his society.'

'a personal and dynamic relationship between two people ... with mutual consideration for each other ... to the end that [one] is aided to a self-determined resolution of his problem.'

'a counsellor helps [the other] to marshal his own resources ... to achieve the optimum adjustment of which he is capable.'

'a permissive relationship which allows [the counsellee] to gain an understanding of himself [and so] take positive steps.'

'a conversation or series of conversations between two persons ... to resolve the conflicts, reduce the anxiety and/or modify ... response. Counselling is obviously a learning situation.'

'Talking, listening, sharing, caring, complex, asking the right questions and allowing the client to come up with solutions to what are perceived as problems.'

'To get people to look at things from a different angle/perspective.'

So, what is counselling?

Counselling is a way of responding and relating to someone so that they feel clearer about what is concerning them. They then feel better able to help themselves and make their own decisions. It helps them to talk about, and work out what their feelings are, before taking any action. It is this *exploration and understanding,* before action, which is special about counselling.

There are many definitions of counselling. All of them agree on the basic principle that *counselling is about helping clients to help themselves.* This is important, because most of us have difficulty, to a greater or lesser degree, in taking responsibility for our own lives. *The concept of personal responsibility is at the heart of the counselling process.* Taking responsibility demands a high level of self awareness. This means that you have to understand yourself, and your reasons for behaving in a particular way in particular situations. This understanding is one of the outcomes of the counselling process. You need this understanding of why you do things before you can change the behaviour.

■ Behavioural counselling

There is a school of thought called behavioural counselling which uses reward as a means of acquiring or strengthening behaviour, and this will sometimes achieve a change. However, because you do not know why you behaved that way in the first place, it is very probable that the same behaviour you have tried to change will reoccur. Also, because the reward is external and specific, the results are specific to that piece of behaviour.

Here is an example of a manager trying to help a subordinate who was finding it very difficult to control team meetings.

Subordinate I don't know what I'm doing wrong, but I never seem to be able to get through all the agenda items. When a discussion starts, I don't know how, but it seems to take over.

Manager You mustn't let them take control. You have to let them know who is running the meeting. What you have to do is strictly monitor the agenda, time discussions and keep strictly to the allotted time and subjects. By doing this, you will regain control of the meetings.

The subordinate is clearly at a loss to know what takes the meetings 'out of control'. The advice his manager gives him is very sound, but does not help him understand what is going wrong. If he does not know what it is about meetings that makes him lose control, any instant solutions will be short-lived. So it is not that the advice is incorrect, it is like curing the symptoms of a disease without knowing the cause: the chances are you may not cure it, or it may reoccur. If, however, you can understand the reasons for acting in a particular way in particular situations, the potential for change, and permanent change is far greater.

With a broader understanding of yourself, you can react far more effectively to internal and external forces in order to achieve goals and meet needs.

■ The counselling relationship

For the purposes of this book, we will be viewing counselling as a 'repertoire of skills', used to establish and maintain a supportive relationship. This relationship is essentially *'non-directive'* and aimed at *'empowering'* the client. This means that it does not involve the counsellor telling the client what to do, but rather to help the client come to an understanding of their situation, and come to their own solutions about what they will do.

The counsellor's skills include those of forming relationships, and skills focused on helping the client to change specific aspects of their thinking, feeling and behaviour.

Counselling is not only about helping people through difficult situations, it is about developing capabilities and releasing creative energies. It is a very positive and productive action, rather than an activity that goes on when people are in trouble. This is a side of counselling that is rarely emphasised, and it is one which has considerable significance for the manager.

You may want to use counselling to help someone realise talents and skills you have spotted but they have not. For example, you may have someone on your team who you feel has the potential to take on a new post with more responsibilities. They may feel inadequate to do this. Telling them will not make them feel able to do it. It is not enough to say to someone that they are wonderful; they have to realise it, understand it, and accept it themselves. This acceptance can be achieved through the counselling process.

Counselling also helps release tension, which can block a person's ability to create and function normally. This is possibly the most frequent occasion when a manager will feel it appropriate to counsel. For example, take the case of Janet, an editor in a publishing company. She was very bright, vivacious and full of ideas. She was always happy to work on her own initiative, and set her own goals and deadlines. She was extremely successful, and was left to manage on her own. When she had her first child, she took off three months and came back to work. At first no one seemed to notice any difference in her work. However, after about three weeks, her manager noticed that she was being very abrupt with her team, and was unable to give them instructions or guidance in their work.

When the manager talked to Janet about it, she lost her temper, and said that a huge pile of work had accumulated while she was away, and how was she supposed to cope with the volume of work with such an undisciplined team? This was not the kind of outburst that her manager would have associated with Janet.

She broached the subject with Janet, who said that everything felt too much for her. They agreed that much of Janet's anger was due to her perceived inability to function at her previous level, without allowing for the extra, unusual pressure that Janet was under, because of the baby.

After a counselling session, they agreed that Janet was not functioning to her normal level because of external circumstances, and she needed some support to help her 're-entry' to work. The manager agreed to provide Janet with some structure, and give Janet deadlines instead of Janet setting them herself. They agreed to review the situation in six months.

At the end of that time, Janet was beginning to function almost to her normal level, and they agreed that Janet could now begin to put back her own structures. Within a year, Janet was working on her own, and producing her normal standard of work. What Janet had needed was someone to help her identify what was going wrong, and help her sort out a means of dealing with it. Her manager gave her the time and the 'space', and was rewarded with a fully functioning member of staff.

■ Coping with change

Counselling has a role in facilitating change and adapting to change. This role can be twofold: to help someone adjust to a change, and also to help support and maintain the change. Examples of changes are redundancy, career change, personal circumstances, role change; these are all times when counselling might prove a useful tool for the manager .

Having established how vital counselling is to the manager, why is it such a neglected skill? Let's look at some of the myths and misconceptions that surround counselling:

It takes too long.
I don't have time for all that nonsense.
Fear of stigma – am I ill?
Cultural fear of discussing personal issues.
Nobody's business but my own.
I have to work it out on my own.
How will others see me?
Will it affect my promotion prospects?
Only wimps (or women) need to talk things through.
Will it change me?
Will it make me talk about things I don't want to talk about?.

These are all things people actually have said when faced with the counselling process. These thoughts come from managers and staff members, and seem to fall into three major categories:

1. That it is a lengthy and time consuming process.
2. That it is culturally 'not OK'.
3. That they do not know the outcomes and effects of the process at the outset.

Let's look at these categories individually:

Argument	Response
• That it is a lengthy and time consuming process. • It takes too long. • I don't have time for all that nonsense.	*This is a 'How long is a piece of strings?' question. It also begs the question 'What will be the effect of you doing nothing?' It need not be a lengthy process. Sometimes all people need is a bit of 'space', and the time to verbalise their situation to clear their heads, and enable them to act. This could be anything from five minutes to five weeks. Sometimes just the knowing that there is someone you can talk freely to is enough.*

All managers should be able to provide this forum for talking for their staff. This is a counselling skill. The level to which they develop the forum is down to each individual manager. However, this forum does not appear automatically, neither does it become yours with the title of 'manager'. You have to create an environment that encourages people to speak freely. Once this is established, the time will vary with each situation.

Some managers say that they are approachable, that their door is always open, that people can always talk to them. The need to announce this gives the lie to the statements. If they are true, then people will know. Very few managers can have their door always open: this is unrealistic. So when the member of staff comes along and finds the door closed on more than one occasion, that person will not feel able to be honest with that manager, as the manager has not been honest with them. It is not enough to tell people of your intentions. In order for people to believe them, they have to experience them as true. This is part of the trusting, respecting relationship which is central to both management and counselling.

Argument	**Response**
That it is culturally 'not OK'. This is probably the largest group of reactions. It covers thoughts like:	*The British do not like the idea of talking about themselves to someone else. We see it as being weak and self indulgent. Physical problems are OK to*
• Nobody's business but my own.	*discuss, but somehow, we feel that if we*
• I have to work it out on my own.	*have a personal problem, we should be able to deal with it ourselves, and we*
• Will it affect my promotion prospects?	*have no right to even perceive it as a problem. This attitude has lead to the*
• Only wimps (or women) need to talk things through.	*apparent and perceived lack of concern by managers for their staff. If*
• Will it change me?	*you ask someone who they like having*
• Will it make me talk about things I don't want to talk about?	*as a manager, or ask yourself who you have liked having as manager, you*
• Will it change other people's views about me?	*will find that the people you respect the most are not just those who achieve*
• I should be able to work this through myself. I *can't* need counselling.	*their work targets, but those who have done so by involving and listening to their staff.*

Therefore, in order for people to believe that talking to their manager about a problem will not damage their promotion prospects, they have to experience this as being true. If that is not something the manager can promise, he would do better to say so to the staff member. This would leave the responsibility for the problem with the staff member, but leave the staff/manager relationship enhanced by an honest response.

This is part of setting realistic boundaries to work relationships. There are limits imposed on the relationship by the organisation, by the staff member and by you as the potential counsellor. An essential part of counselling is the setting of and keeping to, boundaries. Everyone needs to know how far they can go, and what they can and can't do. This stating of boundaries creates part of the security that is vital to strong, honest and productive relationships. Without the security, people will not feel 'safe' to discuss anything. Saying 'No' and referring people on are all part of the boundary setting. (The actual mechanics of boundary setting and contracting are dealt with in detail in Chapter 8).

Giving a member of staff time and space to talk is one of the most fundamental roles of the manager. Giving time and valuing the member of staff is the easiest way to motivate people, yet it is the least used, in fact it is neglected. This is partly to do with a cultural perception of it being weak to talk , but also with a fear of invading other people's privacy. This is partly a fear of someone invading our own privacy, but we put our own fears onto the client. We have to separate what is our fear, and what is the client's (see Chapter 12).

Argument	Response
That they do not know the outcomes and effects of the process at the outset. • Will it affect my promotion prospects? • Will it change me? • Will it make me talk about things I don't want to talk about? • Will it change other people's views about me?	*There may be fears that talking about a subject will bring people face to face with details about themselves that are unpleasant, or that they do not want to acknowledge. This is a justified fear if something is stopping a member of staff from functioning properly at work, and they do not know what it is, the chances are that it is something that they either don't know about, or don't want to know about (sometimes it might be both). Therefore, counselling might make them talk about things they don't want to talk about and it might change their behaviour.*

The fundamental detail to remember here is that *counselling*, by its very nature, *is a voluntary activity*. No one can 'make' anyone get involved in counselling. It has to be something the client wants to do, as it is they who have to take the responsibility. So, for example, it may not be a 'pleasant' experience for a client to come face to face with the fact that their need to control other people, or that they are perceived by their staff to be bossy and dictatorial. However, without the client's acceptance of the situation, no change can come about. As a manager, you run the risk of long term damage within the team, and work efficiency, if you avoid dealing with conflict.

An important issue to raise here is the limit of the 'manager as counsellor' role. This is discussed fully in Chapter 7, but it is important to say here that any counselling the manager does at work has a limitation placed on it by virtue of the manager's position and their skills. It is *not* the manager's place to indulge in amateur psychotherapy.

■ The principles of counselling

So, having looked at some of the issues around counselling, what are the principles of counselling itself?

There are four underlying tenets of counselling.

1. That it is *real*, and not rooted in fantasy, and is about helping to deal with reality.

2. That it demands *empathy*, which is the ability to understand someone else's frame of reference. This means being able to interpret another's tone of voice and vocabulary, *as they are meant by that person*. This obviously demands very good listening and observation skills, and an ability to understand the other person's feelings, even when they are badly expressed. Sympathy is a very different feeling, and in terms of

moving people on, is a passive, non productive emotion. Empathy, by contrast is a complex and active emotion which involves both the counsellor and client. It can be defined as feeling *with* someone as opposed to feeling *for* someone. It means getting into someone else's head while staying in your own. Understanding someone else's framework, and exactly what they mean when they use particular words or phrases, and not imposing your personal interpretation.

Because understanding empathy is such a fundamental part of the counselling process, it might be helpful to illustrate the difference between empathy and sympathy with an example:

Client: I'm terrified about doing that presentation tomorrow.
Counsellor (sympathetic) Oh dear, I know just how that feels. Don't worry, you'll be OK.
Counsellor (empathic) What is it that makes you feel so nervous?

3. That it demands *acceptance* of the person and situation without judgement. This means that whatever feelings, expressions or sentiments the client expresses, the counsellor will not pass judgement on them, but put them into the context of the person and situation. This is one of the most difficult principles of counselling to adhere to, as it asks the counsellor to put aside what may be very deeply held beliefs and values for the length of the consultation. Without this acceptance, however, the client will not feel secure enough to disclose their deeply held beliefs and values, for fear of disapproval. Without this acceptance, there can be no empathy, and therefore no true understanding of the client's needs, fears and hopes.

4. That the counsellor must be able to '*let go*'. This means allowing the client to identify, explore and make their *own* decisions about their situation. Again a difficult task for the counsellor, since their desire is to help the client, and it frequently seems easier to tell them what to do, particularly if they ask! (This is largely to do with the counsellor's motivation to counsel, and is discussed more fully in Chapter 7.) The aim of counselling is to enable the client to be aware of, feel in control of, and take responsibility for, their particular situation. This is called 'owning' the problem or situation. This means that the situation belongs to the client, and it is the counsellor's role to help them gain and maintain ownership. One of the most important roles for a counsellor is that of an objective observer, who can see things the client cannot, because they are outside the situation. As soon as a counsellor loses their objectivity, they will be unable to help the client. Having helped the client to own the situation, the control over what happens in the situation remains with the client. Without this ownership, the control of the situation will pass to the counsellor, which will not in any way help the client. It is this 'letting go' which stops the counsellor feeling overwhelmed and 'involved' with the client.

This particular tenet of 'letting go' may be an issue for managers who are promoted because they are dynamic and forceful, and push others around. If you feel that you need to be very directive, you need to assess whether the situation genuinely demands a directive approach (and many do), or whether it is *you* who demands a directive approach. Neither of these are counselling.

Advice is directive and is not counselling. Giving advice implies you know more than the client and are therefore better equipped to make decisions about the client's situation. It takes the power away from the client, and whose problem is it, anyway?

Advice and sympathy and information-giving all go straight to solutions without exploration. It is this exploration which is special and productive about counselling.

6·Where Counselling Can Help

■ Summary

In this chapter, we look at some of the situations that may give rise to counselling. A 'good' manager will be able to recognise patterns of behaviour which might be dealt with by counselling. Although it is not possible to predict people's behaviour with certainty, there are some situations which will cause problems for most people, most times they occur. It is also true that certain issues, such as changes in the work environment or personal life, will have an effect on people's work performance.

The three main types of situation that arise are:

- Issues from the organisation.
- Issues from the individual's own personality.
- Issues from the individual's external environment.

So situations occur at work, triggered off by events both at work and outside of work, that result in differences in an individual's behaviour. When this results in a loss of productivity and/or well-being of an individual, or of a group, it is the manager's role to assess the situation, and deal with it appropriately.

■ Case study: Ted Bridges

Consider the case of Ted Bridges, production manager of a large modern brewery. He can well remember the culture shock when he took up his present job. He was proud to be selected by his firm to leave the old fashioned brewery he had been running in the heart of a Midlands city and join the inaugural team on the company's new production flag ship. He received technical updating and came to grips with the changed technology without much difficulty. But he had not foreseen the tremendous challenge the new environment would present to his style of management. Hitherto he had successfully managed large teams of men with traditional skills and work patterns. He was out in the brewery most of his day in a lively atmosphere, always surrounded by people. He had understood exactly what everyone was doing and this mastery, combined with a concern for high standards and a friendly approach, had gained him his staff's respect and co-operation.

The new brewery is out in the country with most of the staff living in a small village nearby – the only village for miles around. The brewery is vast with surrealistic towers linked by long pipes and walkways. At different locations small groups of technicians work quietly watching instrument panels. Ted himself now spends much time in his office receiving and responding to information and is otherwise often walking from one location to another along empty walkways. A grasp of the technology did not, he soon discovered, mean an instant understanding of what to do if things went wrong. All the expertise contained in his small technical teams might have to be drawn upon to resolve what might initially seem a small problem. He could no longer just give an order. He had to sit down and review the data, consult everyone and often rely on a subordinate's specialist knowledge in reaching a conclusion. At first he thought this situation was due to teething troubles; now he is beginning to recognise it as a permanent feature of the new job.

Personal relationships within teams and between himself and his staff have become much more important. In the old brewery the pace and physical nature of the work had helped to reduce antagonisms, and the number of people about had ensured that no-one needed to work in the unrelieved company of someone they found antipathetic. When people left work at the end of the day, they went out into a busy city and dispersed to homes in many different locations.

In the new brewery all these conditions are reversed. Ted's staff work closely together on tasks which demand mental concentration over long periods. When they leave work they drive to the village where their spouses and families are still adjusting with varying success to an isolated life in a small community. Although the villagers are no longer wary of the newcomers, it could not be said that many friendships have sprung up. Ted realises that both work efficiency and individual job satisfaction could suffer sharply if personal relationships go sour. He finds himself having to listen and understand as never before. The strain is considerable and seems to be affecting him more and more.

■ Case study: Mary Ellington

Consider the case of Mary Ellington, brought in to take charge of the computer department in a medium-sized engineering firm. In her late twenties, Mary had considerable experience working in a range of mainframe computer systems, while her hobby as a voluntary supervisor in a sports centre had given her some experience of management. But this is her first post as a manager and she is the first woman the firm had appointed to such a level.

Although very proud of her new job, Mary has encountered some problems. Her immediate boss understands the department's work but is immensely busy and often away on business trips. The director to whom he reported and to whom Mary reports in his absence knows little of computer technology; his demands on the department showed this and some of the department staff are openly highly critical of him.

The computer system used in the department is in some respects new to Mary, but particularly with her boss away so much, she is for many months too busy to settle down and learn it as thoroughly as she might have wished. She still feels she is having to catch up. Then, although most of the department staff were friendly from the beginning, two experienced male operators made it plain that they had each wanted her job. They lost no time in telling her that she was inadequately qualified. One in particular continues to imply that a woman should not be in the post and that she should get herself a decent boyfriend and stay home.

Some of these problems have eased with time and the work continues to be very interesting. She has gained people's respect and trust and the firm now relies on her. But some things do not change; the workload remains heavy and the long hours have greatly curtailed her leisure time. She does have a boyfriend and he points out that they now have much less time together and she seems to put her job before him.

She remains very isolated at work. After two years she has concluded that she will not be able to change these adverse features and also that she is unlikely to be promoted further. With nobody in the firm to talk to, she is beginning to listen to the headhunters who phone her from time to time pointing out where else she could be employed.

■ Case study: Hugh Cattermole

Consider the case of Hugh Cattermole, a competent 53-year-old insurance manager. He works as second-in-command in a country office of what was until recently a successful medium-sized insurance company. Hugh has kept up with modern technology and uses his own personal computer. He is respected and trusted by his older staff and his clients and in his local community. His three children have now all left home and are in good jobs in London.

Last year Hugh's firm was taken over by a much larger insurance company seeking to extend its coverage of provincial areas. He tried to view this development positively and to welcome the wider experience and new ideas it might bring. But actually what he experienced was a growing number of rules and constraints on how he was required to operate. There was also increasing pressure to develop more business at the price, it seemed to him, of customer service. However, he continued to work hard, indeed to work longer and longer hours, and looked forward to taking over the office when his boss retired. And then two things happened. The board of the major company in which he is now employed, decided on a policy of office rationalisation and the development of a more youthful image to help attract scarce graduate recruits. Hugh's office was given notice of closure and the staff were told they would be transferred to another of the company's offices at the other end of town.

Hugh's boss decided to take early retirement but Hugh has not been promoted. Instead, a younger member of staff has taken over and Hugh has been offered a job which is, effectively, a demotion.

Meanwhile, he is facing difficulties at home. Before her children were born, Hugh's wife was a buyer in a large department store. She loved her work and always said she would try to go back to it once the children were launched. Once they had left home she began to look around. She has now accepted an interesting job in her brother's shop some 200 miles away, and proposes to stay with him during the week and 'see how it goes'. She points out that, especially with Hugh working longer and longer hours, home for her is now just a lonely round of boring domestic chores. She says it is high time she started living for herself again. Hugh feels unable to cope with these experiences and is becoming increasingly withdrawn and unresponsive both at work and at home.

* * *

Ted, Mary and Hugh are all valuable employees and Ted's and Mary's employers, at least, know how valuable they are. But all three of them are now subject to considerable strains due to the cumulative effect of major social and technological developments operating in combination with doubtless sound management decisions. The result is that two of them are gradually becoming less effective while Mary is deciding to leave. Their stories are not unusual and many of their colleagues will have undergone similar experiences and share some of their feelings.

■ The case for counselling

Enlightened self interest should be enough to interest employers of such staff in ways of relieving the strains they experience. Among the measures they could consider, counselling must surely come high. Whether or not the wider circumstances can be changed, counselling can help individuals to make constructive moves to ease their own situation or at least to accept what must be accepted. It can speed the process of coming to terms with change and check the development of damaging reactions which rebound upon other staff. In these terms, counselling is not a luxury service nor even a humane element in a good personnel programme, but simply sound business practice.

The circumstances which are affecting employees such as Ted, Mary and Hugh are by now well known. Our population structure has changed and jobs have changed. Technology has altered the skills we need and the conditions under which we work. New attitudes to careers and family life are affecting everyone in employment. If the full implications for employment of the political changes in Europe have scarcely been envisaged, at least we all know that 1992 is going to alter the labour market dramatically.

But, in general, the challenge of adapting to these changes has been considered in terms of policies and practices, rather than impact on individuals. We have some idea of what we should be doing about recruitment (ie the opposite of what many companies are now doing, which is to engage in an increasingly expensive scramble after graduates) and about training and retraining and the analysis of job skills and competencies. Companies have accepted some responsibility for easing the pains of redundancy and relocation. But we have paid less attention to the strains which demographic and technological changes are imposing on those remaining in employment, who are expected to see the organisation through the white rapids into calmer water.

■ The importance of good staff

There are many problems a manager has to deal with. These range from cashflow, to production issues. Underlying all of them, are the staff the manager needs to deal with the problem. It is this side of problem solving that is neglected. A great deal of time is spent on strategic decision making, but disproportionately little time on the people who will have to implement the decision.

There is also a tendency to concentrate on people's technical skills, as opposed to interpersonal skills. Of course technical skill is essential, but *people do not work in a vacuum*. There are other people around, both in the workplace, and in their private lives, and they affect the way people work.

A 'good' manager learns through experience, and is able to recognise patterns of events and situations which could lead to problems. With individuals, however, this is somewhat more difficult, because no two individuals are the same. It is therefore difficult to 'predict' behaviour with the same certainty as you might predict computer problems.

There are numerous theories on behaviour prediction, ranging from Freud to John Hunt (for further information on these areas, see suggested reading). Freud, for example, felt that there were two important factors in the formation of groups and organisations:

- *Issues with leadership*. The group cannot form unless a leader has been established and accepted.
- *Issues with relationships*. Once everyone accepts the leader, they then have to agree their common focus, and their working relationships.

Professor Hunt felt that various circumstances and values created people's motivation to work. If these circumstances or values changed, or were forced to change, then it would have an effect on the individual's behaviour. For example, if it was important for someone to work as part of a team, and they were suddenly told that they would now be working on their own, this would probably have a marked effect on their work.

These are among the many theories. Whilst they are theories, they seem to be borne out by experience, and it is worth your while to do some background reading, in order to gain insight. This book cannot cover everything in detail.

■ People issues

There seem to be three types of people issues.

- Issues coming from the organisation
- Issues coming from the individual's own personality
- Issues from the individual's external environment

restructuring, promotion, demotion, policy changes.

individual behaviour patterns.

moving, marriage, loss.

Most people suffer problems of one kind or another. They are like the common cold of the emotions. When they arise, there are three common elements:

- A difficult situation.
- A fundamentally 'normal' person.
- The failure of the normal psychological mechanisms the individual normally uses to handle such situations.

In other words, there are some situations which would upset most people. It is the counsellor's role, to distinguish between transient problems, and those of a more disabling nature. For example, is the problem the client is experiencing one which is situational, and they will be able to deal with in the course of time? Or is it more serious, in that the client is stuck, and cannot understand why the situation is so difficult for them? People experiencing a 'situational disturbance' cannot quite tell what is wrong, although they do recognise behaviours that are not characteristic of them. The counsellor has to be careful not to give mere reassurance, as this might undermine the person. They also have to beware of overdiagnosis of a situation – it is not as bad as the counsellor is making out. Once again the counsellor is obliged to listen. Listen to the context in which the incident(s) occurs. Is this isolated? Has it happened before? Have they dealt with it before? Are the circumstances different? And so on.

■ Individual differences in behaviour

One of the mysteries of life is the fact that people carry on, despite enormous emotional and psychological burdens. Some individuals can handle severe blows to their self esteem, and still come back with confidence. Others find everything a struggle, and the slightest thing can throw them off beam, so that they cannot continue with everyday activities.

Past experiences are also a good guide to people's reactions. Those who have suffered 'the slings and arrows of outrageous fortune', and have learned the hard way about the way life can give or take away things that are sought after, are generally better equipped to deal with change. Ordinary stresses of life are easier to cope with if there are some options, or available solutions. Most people cope better with choices. It is when the choices are removed that stress has its greatest effect (see Chapter 4).

When someone is going through some situational problem, the chief reaction is anxiety, although it takes many forms. These range from restlessness, irritability, and an inability to concentrate, to a preoccupation with detail. They sometimes go through physiological symptoms of anxiety; for example, loss of sleep, tiredness, under-eating, over-eating.

Sometimes people are surprised by new events or behaviours in their lives and they resort to activities which compound their problems. For example, someone who gets into fights at work, in order to deal with problems at home.

Despite the fact that a person's behaviour might stem from any one or more of these categories, the presenting behaviours are likely to be the same. For example, if someone is very preoccupied with moving home, their disinterested behaviour at work might be similar to someone who is having difficulty dealing with their workload, because it is beyond their capability.

What situations might prompt a need to counsel staff?

* People not performing to their usual standard.
* Persistent lateness.
* Inability to communicate clearly.
* Inability to act as part of a team.
* Unusual, or changed behaviour.
* Inability to take or make decisions.
* Change in personal circumstances.
* Change in work circumstances.

What sort of issues might they bring?

* Marital problems
* Bereavement
* Drinking
* Drugs
* Health
* Emotional adjustment
* Inability to cope
* Lack of skill/ability
* Career crisis
* Personality problem

So what kinds of behaviours might signal to you a need for counselling?

* Eager to please, wants to help rather than do, looking for a friend, cannot accept success, constantly worries about failure, dependent on others, indecisive, avoids responsibility, always taking on new work, never completes to deadlines, constantly at meetings.

* Aggressive, talks at you, does not listen, bosses others, obstinate, fixed views and opinions, autocratic, unwilling to delegate, critical and contemptuous of others, unreasoned, envious, cannot take criticism.

* Cannot organise own work properly, blames others constantly, finds it difficult to finish jobs, defensive, secretive, has few friends, irrational, prone to panic, avoids personal contact, uncooperative, sometimes deprecating about the organisation, uses memos, puts off work, anxious.

All of these are behaviours, or symptoms, of an issue that has to be dealt with. It is not exhaustive, but raises some of the potential times when counselling may be appropriate. However, it is not just the issues which determine whether counselling is the appropriate path to take; we need to look at the circumstances and the manager's own position when deciding how to deal with the situation.

7·The Role of the Counsellor

■ Summary

In this chapter, we look at the qualities of a 'good' counsellor, and compare them to the qualities of a 'good' manager. There are none that do not apply, although there are other skills that a manager does have to learn. However, the skills of people management and leadership revolve around the ability to make people successful and productive. Counselling belongs within this group of skills. It is also important to look at the reasons why some managers choose to counsel, and what clients find attractive about counsellors. There are many managers who choose not to counsel. Whatever their reasons for making this choice, and it might be that this is a personal limitation, the importance of counselling as part of the manager's role cannot be diminished. Discussing issues which will benefit the employee is not necessarily against the company interest. Although the organisation's purpose in life is not to satisfy their employees' needs, the well-being of their staff will be reflected in the company productivity.

A 'good' counsellor:

- Understands why they are counselling.
- Knows their personal limitations.
- Knows their professional limitations.
- Has an understanding of why people come to them.
- Knows what skills and techniques they need to help the client.
- Can progress understanding to action.
- Respects and accepts their clients.
- Can negotiate appropriate boundaries of confidentiality.

■ What is a good counsellor?

A 'good' counsellor:

- Is aware of their own feelings, and knows themselves.
- Is aware of their own intellectual abilities.
- Is imaginative in their approaches.
- Is comfortable and skilled when dealing with emotions – both their own and others.
- Respects their clients.
- Can integrate feeling, experience and behaviour.
- Is at home with people, in a one to one situation or in groups.
- Can progress understanding to action.

The counsellor needs to understand their own reactions, before they can understand others. They need to be aware of their own abilities and parameters. They need to be open to change and new thought. They need to be able to turn theories into practical ideas, that can help them to help others more effectively. They need to be able to help people put together their feelings, experiences and behaviour into an understandable framework. They need to able to accept, and not judge. They need a wide range of interpersonal skills, but they also need the insight to know when to use them. They need to know when to listen and when to speak; when to invite and when to close down; when to watch and when to tell.

If this sounds like Superperson, it is. This is one version of an ideal. We do not live in an ideal world, and most people will fall short in one way or another at various different times. However, without an ideal, it is difficult to focus on a direction to be aimed for.

Which of these descriptions does *not* apply to the 'good' manager? **None. The skills of people management and leadership revolve around the motivation and ability to make people successful and productive.** Counselling belongs in this group of skills.

There is a fear that as counsellor, the manager will lose 'power'. Most of the time the manager is responsible for decision-making, accepting responsibility for results, and using their charisma. As the manager, you possess the problem. The manager's role in counselling is to empower the client, and the client possesses the problem. This does not mean that the manager is powerless, it means that they have to take a different role. The actual shift for the manager is not in the qualities required, but in the role required.

■ Critical issues

What sort of issues bring out the role conflict for the manager as counsellor?

- Decisiveness.
- Time pressures.
- Assessing line management issues.
- 'Extra work, little results'.
- Company culture.
- Personal style.
- Confidentiality.

Decisiveness

The company demands that the manager makes and takes decisions. It is impressed upon the manager that he or she must at all times be decisive. On management training programmes it is posssible to get managers to the stage where they are actually listening to what people are saying. However, as soon as you put them in any kind of work simulation, which demands a result, for most of them, the listening disappears and the task-oriented manager reappears. It seems to be perceived that you cannot make decisions through listening!

Time pressures

The manager and the external counsellor may have different objectives. The manager may feel that an issue needs to be resolved instantly, and it doesn't matter whose intervention solves the problem. An external counsellor may feel they have the time to let the client sort things out for themselves. Solving issues within a time limit, and using counselling techniques to solve a problem, are not mutually exclusive. Evaluating and improving performance does not mean telling them how to do it. It means helping someone find the best solution and commit themselves to it.

Assessing line management issues

A manager will often have to decide whether a client is bringing a request for the manager to act, or a request for help. Take the case of Jeff Warner.

Jeff was a project leader in a computer software company. He came to his manager and requested an extension on a project deadline. His manager had to assess whether:

- Jeff was giving him prior warning so that the manager could prepare himself, and reorganise connecting issues.
- Jeff could not organise or delegate tasks to his team properly, and so the work was not done.
- Jeff was not equipped to deal with the task, and was using the change of deadline to avoid facing this.
- Jeff was able to do the job. However, he was absorbed temporarily by personal issues, which were affecting his ability to do the job.

If the manager makes an assessment without finding out the facts, they potentially risk not only missing their deadline, but also the opportunity to help a subordinate function properly.

'Extra work, little results'

It is a lot easier for the manager to tell Jeff that he must pull himself together and meet the deadline, than to deal with a potential problem which the manager may not be able to deal with themselves. If there is a performance problem, the manager may first have to convince Jeff that he has a problem. It might just be yet another issue he has to deal with. All this might just make the manager feel that they would rather deal with it themselves.

Company culture

Sometimes the manager themselves may be a caring individual, but the company may have certain taboos about 'caring' behaviours. This might mean that even if the manager wanted to help, they would not be encouraged or supported by the company, and it might even damage their future prospects. This would only mean them setting themselves up for frustration.

Personal style

Sometimes this is not so much a conflict of role, as a personal conflict. For example, some managers do not feel that they have a genuine warmth for others. This might be due to shyness, inadequacy or an 'uncomfortable' feeling when discussing emotions.

Confidentiality

Confidentiality is an issue of prime importance to clients. People often find it difficult to talk about themselves and are likely to find it even more difficult if they feel that the discussions will be disclosed.

So whose confidentiality is it? To whom does the interview material belong? To the counsellor and client alone? To the counsellor and their superior? To the counsellor and their manager? To the external counselling agency and the personnel department?

There is no easy answer to these questions. Each case is different. What is consistent, however, is that a contract of confidentiality must be agreed between counsellor and client, and the boundaries agreed, and adhered to.

■ Confidentiality

In courts, counsellors cannot claim privilege over matters disclosed to them by clients. It might be easier if there were such plain boundaries in the workplace! Where counsellors are working in settings where there are significant limitations on confidentiality, this fact must be shared with the client from the beginning.

If, in the course of an interview, the client discloses information which might legally compromise the counsellor, then it is necessary for the counsellor to renegotiate the whole issue of confidentiality with the client.

Example

Joseph had been with his organisation for five years as a financial controller, with specific responsibility for petty cash and reimbursement expenditure. He asked to see his manager about what he described as 'a pressing matter'.

Joseph I need to talk to you, but you must promise not to tell anyone.

The counsellor is now being asked to 'collude' with Joseph. It is very flattering to be told 'secrets', or be 'the only one who knows'. However, it is unlikely that the counsellor has the power to give Joseph the complete confidentiality he requests. Why is he requesting it? In a situation like this, there is only one response for the counsellor to make:

Counsellor I cannot promise that, without knowing more about the situation. It may not be within my power to give you that promise.

By saying this, the counsellor has set a boundary, and the reponsibility is back with the client. Joseph was trying to make a 'confession', which he would not have to do anything about. He would, however, feel better for telling someone, and the counsellor would be left holding the problem. Joseph was under severe financial and emotional pressure at home. He had been taking money from the petty cash and 'adjusting' the books. He was desperate to tell someone, but terrified he would lose his job. He therefore tried to use the confidentiality of the counselling interview to protect himself. The counsellor stated at the beginning of the conversation that this was not an option, by refusing to give him carte blanche confidentiality. The discussion continued, and with the counsellor's perseverance, Joseph eventually 'confessed', and accepted that he was going to have to 'confess' officially, and accept the consequences.

However, for most managers, the issue is not always as clear cut. The manager has potentially divided loyalties:

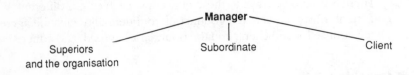

Employers have a legitimate interest in their employees' performance. If therefore, an employee is not performing well, and a manager counsels that employee to find out the reasons for this, why should the company not know of the consequences?

The answer to this incredibly complex problem lies in the nature of what is reported back to the company. All the organisation needs to know is how the employee is going to improve, and what steps will be taken to ensure improvement. In this case, the company need only know the outcome of Stage 3 of the interview. This is not as threatening to the client as the company knowing every intimate detail of the conversation.

There is no blanket answer to the question of divided loyalties, or role conflict. It constantly occurs when a manger is involved in internal counselling. Sometimes the manager sorts it out for themselves, while on other occasions, it may become too complex, and it might be appropriate for the manager to refer to an external counsellor.

Counselling means dealing with the way people relate to one another. A 'good' counsellor is likely to be a 'good' manager, and it is in the organisation's interest that managers understand, support and encourage their staff.

However, work pressures and conflicts of personality frequently work against this. There is often fear and apprehension between manager and subordinate. It is not realistic to counsel someone in an atmosphere of fear and suspicion. This is a boundary for the role of the counsellor as manager. You need to be able to accept this, and either refer the client to an alternative internal source, for example, personnel, or to an external counsellor.

■ What makes a manager want to counsel?

A need to 'do things to and for others'

Doctors and other professionals do things to or for their clients. This is not appropriate in the counselling role. It makes the counsellor the most powerful person, as they have the 'ability to do', and therefore prevents a reciprocal relationship. Some counsellors take on this excessive responsibility. Why?

Individuals who want to do something for the client are creating an inappropriate environment. Frequently, what they want to do for others, they would like to do themselves, but for various reasons, cannot or will not. They may counsel to fulfil needs of their own or fulfil some expectation of their own. This style will probably be ineffective, because it is dealing with their own needs, and not the client's.

You cannot change other people's personalities (short of a lobotomy!). Neither can you change their experiences. You cannot even keep them from making mistakes or 'bad' decisions. You cannot provide happy endings. What you can provide is an environment which allows people to take responsibility for their own lives without reproach.

A desire to help people

There is no reason to deny the impulse to help others, or 'do good'. The ability to help someone come to a decision, or an acceptance, is a very strong motivator. It makes you feel good. What we are talking about is something that gives you satisfaction; like seeing a plant you have nurtured come to bloom. The difference is that you are using other people's lives to gain your satisfaction. This is OK, as long as your need to help does not overbalance the client's need. Your role is to facilitate, not rescue.

You want people to like you

It is not unusual or unreasonable to look for a positive response from the individuals who come to see you. Difficult as it may be to admit this, there are very few people who do not care what people think about them. This issue only becomes a problem if it overrides the client's need. It is necessary to create an environment which encourages people to talk. This only happens when you are concerned about someone else so much, that you cease to worry about whether they like you or not.

One of the most important functions of the counsellor is to create a rapport between the client and themselves. Creating a rapport means supporting an environment that allows a free and honest exchange between counsellor and client. This does not mean that they have to 'be your friend', or indeed that they can be.

A need to judge others

Psychologist Elias Porter has suggested that our need to evaluate others is so much a part of ourselves, that we hardly know it is there. Because it is almost instinctive, this tendency can totally disrupt the non-judgemental nature of the counselling process. This need to evaluate is not the need to form an accurate diagnosis, but a deeper, less conscious need to compare yourself to others, and almost 'grade' your performance and other people's behaviour.

Passing judgement is about putting a value on persons or events. This value is based on *your* perceptions. This judgement is affected by your prejudices, experiences and unconscious motivations. You can see this almost reflex need to be critical in many everyday situations. For example, when you leave a seminar or meeting, the first question that comes to your lips may be, 'Well, what did you think of that?...' The question is not a factual question such as 'What were they trying to put across?' but a more critical question.

In order to get the other person into focus, you have to *suspend judgement*. Too much evaluation also closes down the opportunity to learn about others and about life. If you feel you can put everything and everybody into boxes and categories, not only are you lulling yourself into a false sense of security, but you are limiting your effectiveness. Some of the signs of smugness and over-evaluation can be seen in remarks like: 'What a shame you did that...'; 'Still, it's good that you can tell me these things...'. These are value judgements which do not progress the interview, and indeed may well disrupt it.

A need to give interpretations

This is really about a desire to let the client know (and also yourself), that you do understand what is going on. The unskilled counsellor will frequently use the same interpretation for various situations. For example, they may tell all their clients that they are going through a 'mid-life crisis', and use this 'interpretation' to explain everything.

Skilled interpretation is a crucial part of the counselling process. The timing is extremely important. The risk of premature interpretation is that even though the interpretation may be right, it may be unacceptable because of bad timing. Most people resent having their behaviour interpreted, and can become defensive. Interpretations only work when the client is close to making and accepting those interpretations themselves.

So, while a motivator for counselling might be your need to display your interpretive skills to others, and make you feel powerful, it is unlikely to help the client, and may cause them to withdraw.

A desire to find out about people

This might be subtitled 'human curiosity'. This refers to our curiosity about other people, and how they operate. It can be very exciting to catch a glimpse of someone's private world, and can make you feel very powerful. This is sometimes signalled by over-excessive questioning without space for the client to be heard. Obviously counselling cannot proceed without any questions. It is the way they are asked, and how appropriate they are, that is the key to the counsellor's motivation in asking them.

A need to reassure people

This is one of the most powerful motives for counselling. It is very comforting to feel that you are in a position to 'make people feel better'. One of the most important functions of the counselling process is to be supportive. Being supportive is a very active process. It is not about reassuring noises like 'there, there' or 'don't worry, it will be all right'. This is non-supportive reassurance, and only tells people that they need not feel the way they are feeling. In doing this, it denies their feelings, and devalues their experience. This is *not* constructive support, because if you deny the problem, then you cannot help the client deal with it!

In a more complex vein, some counsellors use the process to reassure themselves, by reassuring others. This goes on at an unconscious level, and occurs when a counsellor has issues of their own they need to resolve. Instead of dealing with the issues themselves, they deal with other people's problems. This sometimes makes them feel that their problems are not so great, or by reassuring others, they are reassuring themselves. This is an important dynamic for the counsellor to be aware of, as it will prevent any work being done with the client.

Real support comes from listening to people as they explore their thoughts, and not backing away when the experience looks like being difficult for you. Giving false or empty reassurance does not help the client or yourself; in fact it increases the counsellor's stress.

Every counsellor, no matter how learned or experienced, has a limit, a personal parameter. This is not about professional boundaries, but more about the recognition of the fact that there is a limit to what you can do. There will be some people you will not be able to help, even with referral.

No-one is expected to succeed all the time. Because you are dealing with human beings, 'success' is far less tangible than how many units you can sell. Personal growth, by its very nature, is limited, and never takes place overnight.

The more you know about yourself, the more appropriate will be your expectations of your performance. People sometimes feel guilty, when they fall short of their ideal. But is their ideal unrealistic? It is important to review realistically the limits of your abilities. What can you actually do for people?

- Can you take away their many experiences?
- Can you change their backgrounds or take away real grief?
- Can you compensate them for bad luck?
- Can anyone remove the obstacles that are found in everyone's life?

You cannot have an answer about your own capacity to help others, unless you are realistic about the things you cannot change. There are some people you can't help, some people who you will never be able to establish a relationship with. This is common sense about people, as well as a reality about your own limitations.

■ Counsellor-attractiveness

What makes people want to be counselled by a particular counsellor?

There are many things that 'attract' clients to counsellors. You may appear attractive because of physical characteristics and appearance; for example, you are good looking and well groomed. You may be attractive due to your position, qualifications or title; for example, personnel, psychologist. Sometimes the attraction is due to a similar experience, or career pattern. Sometimes you are spontaneously attracted to someone, because of a 'bundle' of things, such as age, friendliness, accepting behaviour, admiration. When asked to identify the reasons you might say, 'I don't know why, I just like her.'

These types of attraction, as with the attractions of similar age and interests, can be both attractive, and alienating. They are only helpful to the relationship if they are supported by respect and trust. People may be drawn to you because of your reputation for insight and understanding; this is, through previous clients' reports. It is this reputation for being 'trustworthy' that is the most important, and hardest to define.

Like other counselling skills, being perceived as trustworthy is a crucial management skill. It is this trust that inspires people to work for their bosses, and is a dilute form of charismatic power. Being able to trust your counsellor means:

- *Confidentiality* The client can say: 'Whatever I say to this person about myself, they will not tell anyone else without my permission.'
- *Use of power* The client can feel: 'If I trust this person with myself, they will not abuse that information, and will use it in my interest.'
- *Credibility* The client can say: 'I can believe what he says.'
- *Understanding* The client can feel: 'This person is listening to me, and is trying to understand me.'

The terms for being perceived as 'untrustworthy' are the reverse of these: for example, 'I can't trust them, they always look so untidy and disorganised'. Or, 'You can't trust her, she'll tell your boss everything'.

■ How do you establish trust?

- Make a contract with the client and stick to it.
- Be realistic about the client's, and your own, abilities.
- Provide clients with the kind of structure that makes them feel safe, and thereby allows them to contribute to the 'helping' process. This is part of 'empowerment'. It makes the client feel a part of a process, rather than

someone who is being 'done to'. One way of providing a structure is a clear client counsellor contract. This way both parties know exactly what to expect from the process (for details of contract setting, see Chapter 8).

- Behave in a way which the client can emulate: for example, listening to clients, accepting what they say, communicating understanding. This leads to respect and trust.
- Maintain confidentiality.
- Never promise anything you cannot deliver.

A trusting relationship allows the client to speak more, and feel at ease with the counsellor. The process is circular; encourage the client to speak, and show you are listening, and they will speak more. This is because they trust, and are drawn to, the counsellor.

Generally, clients believe that the counsellor has some information, knowledge, or skill to help them. Sometimes this 'reputation' comes from their role or title, for example, psychotherapist, counsellor. Sometimes the 'reputation' comes from word of mouth, or by association. Neither a role nor a perceived reputation are guarantees of competence.

Sometimes, clients experience the way a counsellor behaves as competency; for example, the language the counsellor uses, or the counsellor's own confidence. These indicators may well be true, but the only evidence for it lies in the actual achievements of the counsellor. They have to be able to deliver whatever they set out to do in the contract. This is where the counsellor's own motivation for wanting to counsel comes into play.

The attraction works both ways, and if a counsellor perceives themselves to be attractive to one client, but not to another, they may tend to be less demanding of attractive clients, and less likely to listen to unattractive clients. The sense of attraction, whether to or from the client, can distract the counsellor from the needs of the client. It might make the counsellor 'perform' rather that listen, or say things they think the client wants to hear, rather than what is appropriate.

Sometimes clients will bring problems that are similar to those of the counsellor. This might affect the counsellor in many ways: they may try and solve their own problem through the client, or hear their perceptions of their own situation, rather than those of the client. Either way, if a similarity of problem gets in the way of the counsellor's ability to help, they should refer the client to someone else.

8·Setting the Boundaries

■ Summary

Setting boundaries at the beginning of the interview is crucial to achieving results. It establishes direction, and allows both the counsellor and the client to measure achievement. It makes explicit the ground rules for the interview, and avoids misunderstanding and false expectations.

- State the parameters of the interview at the beginning of the interview.
- Describe the proposed outcomes, norms and procedures.
- State explicitly the confidentiality and the roles of the counsellor and client.
- Ensure the environment encourages freedom to speak.

Starting a counselling interview is like starting any relationship, whether it is professional or personal. For both people to get the best from the relationship, they need to set guidelines, or boundaries, which describe the type of relationship that each person wants. If these guidelines are not set or discussed, inevitable misunderstandings occur. Setting the boundaries of the interview is the most crucial point of the interview, and covers the following areas:

- What will and won't be covered by the scope of the interview,
- What the interviewee and interviewer should expect as outcomes,
- Length of time of interview,
- Procedure of interview,
- What behaviours are acceptable in the interview,
- Levels of confidentiality,
- Frequency,
- Responsibility.

Without this framework, there is no way of measuring what has been achieved, or indeed focus on the problem. People do not feel secure without boundaries, and will not deem it 'safe' to talk unless they are sure how far they can go, or in what direction they are travelling. This boundary setting is sometimes called contracting, as an agreement or contract has to be agreed by both parties about what they expect and need from the interview. Without this 'contract' you risk raised expectations, false hopes and miscommunication. *The rest of the interview will not flow, proceed or be measurable in terms of results unless an initial contract is set.*

Sometimes people avoid making a contract, as they feel it might inhibit the process, or make the format too rigid. The reverse is true. Too fluid, or lack of a contract makes it difficult to progress. If the terms of the contract change, then renegotiate. (For example, if you begin by saying that everything is completely confidential, and then the client brings up an issue which may require you to involve someone else, then you have to renegotiate the contract terms to accommodate a change in circumstances. If you do not, the relationship will be broken, because you will have broken the contract.)

■ The main boundaries

So having established the importance of boundaries, what are the main boundaries that need to be established at the start of an interview?

- Outcomes.
- Confidentiality.
- Role of the counsellor.
- Norms of the interview.
- Procedures of the interview.
- Time.

Outcomes

This involves discussion from both parties about what they are expecting as a result of the interview. It will be largely initiated by the interviewer, but must be agreed by the client, in order to avoid misunderstanding. It is at this stage that you should discuss what each person expects from the session. It is important to identify the possible, and eliminate the impossible, for example, that the session is not about cementing friendships. For example:

'At the end of the interview session, the counsellor and client will have agreed on the the appropriate direction for the client's career to take.'

'During the hour we have booked to talk to one another, we will have a chance to analyse the issues that are holding me back, and look at ways of dealing with them.'

Confidentiality

This is a statement about who, if anyone, will hear any outcomes, or information, from the interview. *It must be stated at the outset of the interview.* If there is any change to the status of the parameters of confidentiality, then the boundaries have to be renegotiated.

For example, if a client made allegations of sexual harrassment from a member of staff, in order to investigate them fully, it would probably be necessary to involve other people, as well as the counsellor. This means that the counsellor and the client would have to agree on who else might be privy to the information. If the client did not agree to this, and the counsellor felt that it would not be possible to proceed without input from other people, then they would have to discuss again whether an outcome would be possible without renegotiating the terms of confidentiality (see Role conflict, Chapter 7).

Role of the counsellor

This is an explanation of the role that the counsellor will take during the interview. This establishes two points:

1. *The role of the counsellor as an individual.* If, for example, you are the client's line manager, it is very important to describe any differences between the two roles.
2. The part that the counsellor will take in the discussion. This means indicating to the client that the responsibility for any outcomes of the interview will rest with the client, and describing the 'non-directive approach' (see Chapter 5).

Norms of the interview

This involves describing what sorts of behaviours are acceptable in the interview, if they might be different from the norm that the client might expect. If, for example, swearing, smoking and emotional outbursts are not normally acceptable, but you feel that those behaviours might be appropriate in the counselling interview, you must state it. Like all items in the contract, boundaries should be *explicit*, not implicit.

Procedures of the interview

The interviewer should explain the structure of the interview; what sort of stages the interview will have, and what will happen at those stages in the interview. For example, they might describe the interview in terms of the three stage process;

- That it will begin by discussing and exploring the client's situation, in order to identify the issues that have to be dealt with.
- They will then spend time focusing on the issues, trying to understand and clarify them.

Only after having done this, will the interview be able to move to the third stage, which involves:

- Discussing the options open to the client, to deal with the situation (for more detail, see Chapter 11).

They should also explain what will happen at the end of the interview.

Time

The client should be told how much time they have at that particular session. They should also be told whether any further time is available, and if so, under what circumstances. It is also helpful to say what time you will finish. It is not possible to legislate on how long a counselling session 'should' take. Most professional counselling sessions last an hour. Sessions that go on longer than this, tend to be less and less productive as time goes on. There will be times when you do not need to spend an hour with a client. Gauging time in an interview is very difficult, and it is important to be flexible. While this time does not have to be adhered to rigidly, it is worth remembering as a benchmark.

Once established, the purpose of boundaries is to stick to them. If something is contracted, you must *keep to it and be seen to keep to it*. For example, if you agree to spend an hour, spend it. Like children, adults will test boundaries to see if they really are safe. The only way to change them is to renegotiate the terms of the contract.

The contract has to be stated and *explicit*, not implicit. It may be necessary to restate some of the contract terms at the beginning of any subsequent interviews. During an interview, if the interview strays from its purpose, not only is it useful to have the contract to bring you back to base, it is also a way of ensuring that you don't become involved in inappropriate areas.

Part of the boundary setting is setting the environment for the interview. The most important factors for this are **privacy**, and **security and comfort**.

■ Privacy

The most important environmental element is privacy. 'Counselling', in a diluted form, often takes place in corridors, but any serious work has to be done in privacy. Privacy does not only mean a room with just you and the client in it. Privacy means: confidentiality; no interruptions or distractions; and time.

Confidentiality

If this word keeps occurring regularly in this book, it is with good reason. One of people's greatest fears when they go to talk to someone about an issue, is that 'everyone' will know about it. If they wanted everyone to know about it, they would have told everyone. It is also important to strike a balance between stating and overstating confidentiality to the point where the client feels 'why do they keep stating this? Is there some doubt here?'

The best proof of confidentiality is in the reality. Does anyone other than those people agreed by interviewer and client get to hear of what happened in the interview? If not, than you have the glimmerings of a trusting relationship. However, all too often, particularly in large organisations, people are highly suspicious of what, in the past, may have been empty pronouncements of confidentiality. For this reason they have developed a, sometimes rightly, cynical view of statements of confidentiality. This makes it hard for the interviewer to gain trust. It is essential that the counsellor never promises things they cannot deliver, or promises confidentiality that is inappropriate or not possible. The counsellor does not lose trust by being honest. They gain respect.

The only way to establish confidentiality is to be seen to be keeping your word. This takes time and perseverance, and the old adage that trust is earned, not given, is very important to remember.

No interruptions or distractions

People need to feel that they are being heard and listened to. This means that the interviewer has to keep their mind on the client, and not on themselves. In order to do this, you need not only to create an inviting and welcoming environment for the client, but also to create an environment for yourself whereby you can take the time to deal wholeheartedly with the person in front of you.

This means ensuring that:

- The phone does not ring during the interview.
- You do not look about or out of the window.
- No-one interrupts.
- You do not keep looking at your watch.
- You do not shuffle papers or notes.
- You concentrate on the client.

Time

This means quality of time, not just the fact that you are spending, for example, 30 minutes with this person, (which to some people is almost enough in itself), but also that this 30 minutes will be devoted to this person.

It means seeing them on time, and not keeping them waiting. This not only makes people feel devalued, but also makes them tense.

It means ensuring you have enough time to see them, and that after seeing them you have a few minutes to collect your thoughts before your next appointment, so that you don't spend the last ten minutes of the session thinking about your next appointment.

This becomes very important in the light of something we call 'the hand on the door syndrome'. This describes the event when the client talks and maybe even rambles at great length during their allotted time, but just as they are about to leave the session, with their hand on the door, they tell you what is really worrying them. By doing this, they have given you their problem, without having to do anything about themselves.

By telling you about the problem they feel better temporarily, as they feel they have off-loaded it. However, by doing this they are not dealing with the problem at all, and their relief will only be temporary. If you listen carefully during the last ten minutes of a session, you may sometimes feel the signs of a potential 'off-loading', for example, phrases like 'by the way', 'actually', 'well it doesn't really matter because...'. This syndrome does not by any means occur every time, or even regularly, but it is very important to be aware of it.

So why do they do it? Often it is a means of testing out how the counsellor will react, and to see whether the counsellor has been listening to them. But the major reason is to try to 'dump' the problem somewhere, without having to deal with it.

How do you deal with it? There is only one way to deal with it, and that it is to tell the client what they have done: you have to ask them why they have waited until that time to make such an important point. This, however, is not appropriate if you do not have the time to deal with it there and then. If you do not have the time, then it is best to acknowledge their comments, and say that you will look at them next time you speak together. (And make sure you do!) Whichever option you take, you must acknowledge the comments.

The presenting problem

This gives rise to a very important issue in counselling which is covered in more detail in Chapter 9: the issue of the presenting problem.

When you initially negotiate a contract, it will probably be based on what is called the 'presenting problem'. This means the problem that has either been identified by you, the client, or their boss as something that has to be sorted out. This could be anything from a slackening of performance to an inability to communicate with colleagues. This is known as 'the presenting problem'.

Almost invariably this is not the real underlying problem, but until you have mutually agreed what that is, you will negotiate the initial contract based on the presenting problem. Because the goal posts are likely to change, it is as well to be aware of this at the outset, and be prepared for re-negotiation.

For example, you may have organised a counselling session with someone who said they wanted to discuss their promotion prospects. When you begin talking, however, it transpires that they are feeling terribly under pressure, and can't cope wth their workload. This means you will have to agree this with the client, and agree what you feel can be discussed at that session, and redefine possible outcomes.

■ Security and comfort

The interview has to be seen as taking place in a slightly different atmosphere from discussions about work schedules and costings. For these discussions, it may be your custom to sit behind your desk. This is not the most appropriate way of counselling. Why? Because it can imbue the interviewer with an authority which does not encourage a completely honest atmosphere.

While they see you as the authority figure, it is difficult for a client to see how something they say in this environment will not be 'held against them', because of the power of the authority.

So not only does it place a physical barrier between you and the client, and potentially a psychological one, it also does not encourage an atmosphere whereby the client feels that anything they say will be accepted. All too often, interviewers keep behind the desk because they themselves feel 'safer' there. It is more appropriate to sit in chairs at an angle to the client, so that you are not facing them 'head-on' in an aggressive way.

A great deal has been written about setting up environments and body language (see Chapter 9). While it is important not to overreact, it is equally important not to dismiss it. If you consider personal experiences, you will remember times when you have felt that someone's presence was 'threatening', or that you felt 'comfortable' with a particular situation. These feelings are to do with feeling 'in control' of the situation. Your role as a counsellor is to help the client feel 'in control' of their situation so that they can deal with it. Creating an environment where they feel relaxed is crucial. A simple action like sitting too close, or too far away could destroy that environment.

So we have established the need for a statement of purpose and procedure at the beginning of the interview. How do you do it? *All you have to do is state and agree the terms of the contract with the client at the beginning of the meeting.*

This means stating the terms, and checking these are acceptable to the client. They should be stated baldly, with no frills or apologies, just as they are. This is important, as it is crucial to avoid misunderstandings. Therefore the language should be simple, and the sentences short. (Those rules might easily apply to the whole process of counselling...)

Here is an example of a possible contract:

Timing:	One hour.
Frequency:	Once a fortnight; initially for four sessions.
Purpose:	To review progress on time management.
Method:	Discussion and analysis of critical incidents.
Venue:	Manager's office.
Role of counsellor:	Facilitator – not manager.
Role of client:	Ownership of responsibility.

All matters discussed to remain between counsellor and client only.
No note taking during interview unless by agreement.
After each session, a summary of agreed points to be written up by counsellor, and held by client.

This example covers some of the areas we have been talking about, and puts them into practical terms.

So far we have only looked at contracting in terms of the beginning of the interview. It is important to remember that ending the interview is as important as the beginning. While this is covered in detail in Chapter 11, it is important to remember that you need to restate some of the initial contract. This is not only used as a summary device, to show the client what has happened, it is also a way of proving the necessity of the initial contract, and may also be a time to renegotiate. Without the initial contract as a benchmark, it is impossible to see how far you have come, or how far you have strayed from the initial objectives of the interview.

9·Getting the Story

■ Summary

In this chapter, we look at Stage One and Stage Two of the counselling interview. These are about getting the story from the client, and then establishing and focusing on the real situation. Until the 'real situation' is identified and agreed, you don't know what you are dealing with, and therefore how to deal with it. Getting the story involves listening to and observing the client. It means hearing what the client is really saying, and not what you want them to say. It means getting an accurate drawing of the client, and reflecting it back to them. You need to be able to help the client focus on the issues, and enable them to identify and understand what the situation is really about.

The main skills for the counsellor to use are:

- Active listening.
- Observing.
- Specific, appropriate questioning.
- Reactive and empathic responding.
- Analysing and reflecting.

So now you have set your contract, you're ready to begin. It is important to remember that the counsellor should avoid applying theories in a textbook way. This makes the counsellor anxious to do well, and in doing so, they lose sight of their main purpose, which is the client's needs. The counsellor's biggest strength is their own personality. So look at some of the guidelines, and use your intuition within their framework. Make the guidelines your own.

How do you start? First of all, it would probably be helpful to break down the stages of the counselling interview into three stages. Although we are calling this the counselling interview, it applies to any discussions, whether formal or informal.

There are three stages to the counselling process:

- Getting the story – listening, interpreting, responding.
- Understanding the situation – exploring, focusing, giving feedback.
- Moving on – developing strategies, gaining acceptance.

This chapter deals with the first two stages of the process: getting the story; and understanding the situation. The third stage of the process is dealt with in Chapter 10.

■ Stage One: Getting the story

The counsellor aims to establish a rapport with the client by giving them attention, listening, and responding. Because of the way the counsellor responds, the client is encouraged to explore specifically their thoughts, behaviour and experiences, which relate to the current situation.

In order to get the story, the counsellor needs skills of:

- 'Active' listening.
- Open questioning.
- Observing.
- Non – judgemental responding.
- Reflecting.
- Paraphrasing.
- Summarising.

The client has come to you, and at this stage is unlikely to be clear about what their problem is, or how to deal with it. It is very much the counsellor's role at this stage to help the client tell their story.

This means overriding your instinctive 'automatic sorting system'. Normally, you have picked up a great deal of information about people and events, and you use this information to enable you to respond quickly to situations. In the counselling interview, you need to suspend this instinctive behaviour, to enable you to hear how *the client* perceives the situation. It is *their* perceptions at this stage that are important.

Take, for example, the presenting problem of Howard. Howard has always been a totally devoted worker. His work performance has slumped dramatically recently. Is it because he is trying to do too much? Is he capable of completing his workload? Is his job too big? Is he going through any changes outside of work that might affect his performance? How do you know which is the cause, and will your treatment be different?

Finding out what the problem is marks the first part of a counselling session. Of course you could make assumptions, based on your past knowledge of Howard, but they might be wrong, and you could end up dealing with the wrong problem. The point to remember is that, although the presenting behaviours are similar, the causes may be very different, and may require different approaches to deal with them.

Bearing in mind that this stage is about finding out what the client is there for, the most important skills of this stage are **listening and hearing.**

Active listening

This could be a definition for counselling or management itself. It is at the heart of the counselling process, and without it, it is unlikely that any situation will be sorted out.

'**Active**' **listening** is a set of techniques through which one person can obtain information from another. They can be used by the listener to control the direction and flow of the conversation, and the amount and depth of information disclosed.

Listening is perceived by many to be a 'passive' skill: ie, you are supposed to sit and absorb the information being transmitted, without any input. This is *not* the case. The objective of the listener is to:

- Give the speaker every opportunity to speak.
- Demonstrate interest in what is being said.
- Avoid intruding their own information, interpretations or concerns directly.

Give the speaker every opportunity to speak

Human beings have a kind of 'hierarchy of communications'. This means that in establishing relationships, you have to go through stages in order to develop the relationship further. It is represented as a pyramid:

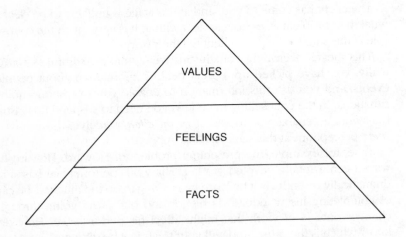

Facts

Most of your relationships in life will not develop past this stage. This is the stage where you only exchange factual information about yourself for factual information about others. For example, the first question we inevitably ask people when we meet them for the first time, is 'What do you do?' The reason why we need to begin with facts is that they are tangible realities, and are therefore unlikely to be threatening in any way. In some way they seem to be 'external' and 'visible'.

Feelings

This is the stage in communication when you can begin to ask questions that relate to how people feel. For example, 'How did you feel when that happened?' People find it too threatening to be asked 'feelings' questions, without first having gone through the 'facts' stage.

Values

This is a stage in the communication process which you will share with a very small number of people. This level of communication concerns your motivation for doing things, the kinds of issues that are important to you, and why they are important. It is this level of communication that provides the counsellor with the 'essence' of the client. You *cannot* bypass the facts and feelings stages and go straight to this stage.

Why?

- They wouldn't tell you.
- It wouldn't make any sense if they did!

If a person says to you out of the blue, 'I've always found it important to tell the truth at all times...', you do not know a great deal more about the person, except the 'value judgement'. You also do not know:

- Whether this is true, as you have no evidence.
- Why it is important.
- The implications that this has for them in their worklife.

That is why it becomes important to use the 'funnelling' technique. If you turn this pyramid upside down, then you have a structure for obtaining information in an interview. This is called a funnel, because you are narrowing down the information until you get the distilled bit at the end of the funnel. In reality, any interaction or interview is likely to contain many 'funnels', as you look for different pieces of information to build up a picture of the person you are talking to.

This funnelling can be best achieved by the type of questions asked. The most appropriate type of question for this stage, is the open-ended question. This is dutifully referred to by most managers as a question which cannot be answered with a simple 'yes' or 'no'.

This is true, but it is also much more than that. It is, as its name suggests, a way of opening up a particular subject area. These questions normally begin with the words, HOW, WHAT, WHY, WHEN, WHERE, WHO. For example:

- 'What sort of projects have you been working on this month?'
- 'How did that affect your relationship with other members of the team?'

THE FUNNEL

• **Start with a general easy open-ended question**
'Tell me about ...'
'What sort of tasks did that involve?'
Check key responsibilities, purpose and outcomes

• **Listen and observe**
• **Follow up**
• **Listen**
Listen for emotive or key words

• **Check factual details**
Ask about what they actually did
'What were your personal tasks on the project?
Get examples

• **Listen**
Suspend judgement
Don't evaluate

• **Learn about feelings**
'What was it like working to a deadline?'

• **Listen and reflect back**

• **Learn about motives**
'What was it you liked
about having responsibility?'

• **Listen**

• **Summarise and seek agreement**

• **Start next topic with a general question**
• **Repeat sequence**

One important aspect of these questions is that all are *specific*: ie, they relate to a particular event or task. This is very important. If a question is put in a vague way, you will receive a vague answer. It is very difficult to answer vague questions any other way! The questions above also help avoid excessive use of 'why' questions. Not only can these sound accusatory, for example:

'Why did you do it that way?'

but also, they are hard to answer because they are abstract. For example, it is quite difficult to answer the question, 'Why do you like your job?', because it is an abstract concept. If you rephrase it to 'What is it you like about your job?', it becomes more specific and concrete, and therefore easier to answer.

Having asked your open question, the next thing to do is *listen to the response. It is the response that is important, not your next question. You do not have to worry about the next question, if you are listening to what the other person is saying.* It will come automatically to you in response to their statement. (If you take nothing else away from reading this book, just practising this behaviour will increase your powers of understanding and perception dramatically.)

It is helpful at this stage to pick up and use the words that the other person is using, particularly emotive words and phrases like:

'I suppose I've been doing all right recently...'

The phrase 'all right' has a multitude of meanings, ranging from 'Absolutely brilliant' to 'Absolutely awful'. It is your role as counsellor to establish what the person means when they use that kind of phrase. Don't shy away from emotive words and phrases. They are the key to understanding your client.

Picking up on words used has a twofold effect: it allows you to understand the client's perspective, and it enables you to show the client that you have been listening to them. This in itself will encourage them to talk further. Having listened and heard what the client is saying, it is time for you to respond. Elias Porter suggests that there are five categories of response:

- Listening and understanding.
- Probing.
- Interpretive.
- Evaluative.
- Supportive.

Listening and understanding

This kind of response is used to reassure the client that they are being heard, and that the counsellor understands the client's point of view. For example:

'It sounds to me as though you are very determined about what you want to do.'

While this may sound like a passive thing to say, it is very important in terms of the client feeling that what they are saying is both understood and accepted by the counsellor. Without these feelings, there can be no progression, as they will not feel 'safe' enough. It is a very constructive feeling to know that what you are saying is not regarded as trivial or silly.

Probing

This is a response which tries to elicit more information from the client, including things that the client may not have thought of. For example:

'I wonder if you thought what effect that might have had on the rest of the team.'

This kind of response, made at the wrong time, ie, too early in the interview, can feel almost accusatory to the client, particularly if it is a closed question. It also takes some of the responsibility away from the client, and almost puts the counsellor in an 'expert' position. This changes the dynamic of the conversation, and it may not encourage the client to feel they have a 'right' to say anything, ie, they may feel inadequate. Probing responses do have a place later on in the interview, at the stage where it is helpful to the client to get a new perspective on the situation.

Interpretive

This is a response which implies an interpretation of the client's comments.

'So that gave you a feeling of superiority.'

At this stage in the interview, you may not have the evidence to make this interpretation. You may sound, like this example, as though you are leading the client. Like the probing response, it may give the power to the counsellor; 'I know something you don't know... Aren't I clever?...'. Again, this response is important later in the interview, when you have a great deal of evidence on which to base your interpretation, and it is necessary to move the client on.

Evaluative

This is a comment which judges what the client has said.

'It would be a great shame if all your work on the project went to waste.'

This has the effect of potentially stopping them talking, as they may feel concerned that they are not saying the 'right' thing. It may even make the client feel angry and defensive. Again it may be useful at a later stage of the interview.

Supportive

This is sometimes a reflex action of the counsellor who feels the client needs an instant solution.

'That must have been awful for you. What you need is a cup of tea and some tender loving care!'

This goes straight to a solution, without checking out the feelings of the client. It may be the wrong solution, and implies that the counsellor knows best. (It may not have been awful!) It also implies that it can be easily sorted out, and that the counsellor will do the sorting. It is also verging on the advice-giving side, which is not counselling. It comes across as a sympathetic comment, ie, feeling *for* someone rather than an empathic comment, which is feeling *with* someone. This again leaves the control with the counsellor, as opposed to the client, and takes away the client's involvement.

It is not that the listening and understanding response is the 'right' one every time, but more that if you introduce the other responses too early in the interview, they may stop the process.

Another important element of giving the speaker every opportunity to speak is to use *silence*. When you ask a question, wait for the answer. Silence does put a great deal of pressure on people to start talking. Make sure this pressure does not operate on you, and that you do not make the silence threatening. You are trying to give them time to think, not put them under pressure. Give them time to think through your question – the more penetrating the question, the more likely it is that the speaker will need a few moments to consider their reply. Silence is a little used, but very power-ful tool. If you do interrupt the speaker's thoughts, they will feel that you are not really interested in their reply, and you will have lost contact. Some-times, a silence can feel overpowering. At these times, it is necessary to ask yourself why it feels overpowering. Is it because you are uncomfortable with the silence? That is not a good reason for breaking it, and says more about you than the speaker. Is it because the speaker is uncomfortable with the silence? That is also not a good reason for breaking it, because it means you are ignoring the reason for their discomfort, ie, something about the question or subject matter has made them feel uncomfortable. It is import-ant that you establish exactly what that is, and why it makes them uncom-fortable. If a silence feels really impenetrable, it may be worth slightly rephrasing the question. If that still has no effect, it is sometimes helpful to actually challenge the silence by commenting on it. For example,

'Are you happy to continue thinking about it?'

Demonstrate interest in what is being said

One way of doing this is by using the funnel technique, and picking up on emotive words. Another way is by using *reflection*. This means taking what the speaker has said, paraphrasing it, and putting it back to the speaker. For example,

Client Everything seemed to be very confused when we changed the planning sys-tem. Everyone was rushing around, without knowing what to do. We were all at a loss as to what we were supposed to be doing.

Counsellor So the change in the planning system upset everyone in the depart-ment, including you. It seems as though you felt that you weren't getting any sup-port or direction from anyone.

The object of this is to show the speaker what the listener has heard. This has a twofold effect:

• It shows the speaker that you have been listening, and more importantly, you have understood what they have said.
• It is a way of holding up to the speaker an image of themselves that they may not be aware they are projecting. By doing this, you are feeding back to the speaker information they can use when assessing their situa-tion.

It is not repeating parrot fashion what the speaker has said; this can be exceptionally irritating. It is taking what they have said, and moving it on to its possible implications:

'When you described the new computer system as confusing, I got the impression that you were finding it difficult to understand.'

Another form of demonstrating interest, and progressing the interview, is by the use of *summaries*. It is very encouraging to the speaker, if the listener gives a short, accurate summary of what has been said. It helps the interaction by:

- Showing that the listener has really been paying attention to the speaker.
- Providing the speaker with a chance to correct any misunderstandings.
- Providing mutually acceptable milestones, from which the interview can progress.

If you don't understand, say so or ask for *clarification* . It is easy to feel that it is your fault if you do not understand. It may even cause you to resent the speaker for putting you in a potentially 'stupid' position. It is much more constructive to use phrases like:

'I'm not sure I understood that. Would you run through it again?'

Note the use of 'I'. It is important that if *you* do not understand, then you must own that feeling and not put it on to the speaker by saying things like 'You're not being very clear'. The use of the word 'I' gives the responsibility for the statement to the speaker, rather than the listener. This avoids the listener getting defensive, and avoiding the issue. It also makes it easier for them to accept their behaviour. This is because they are not being judged on their comments or actions, but rather, someone is making an observation. Managers have a tendency to say things like 'You are being obstinate'. A counsellor might say 'I get the impression that you do not want to change your mind over this'.

Demonstrating interest is not just about verbally responding; it also covers non-verbal behaviour. It is not just receiving what the speaker says, but *how* they say it. Sometimes non-verbal communication may be used to replace language to express emotions, so the listener must *observe* as well as listen.

Signs of attention include:

- Eye contact – but not staring.
- Appropriate smiling.
- Occasional nodding of encouragement (usually accompanied by 'semi verbals' such as 'uh huh', 'go on').
- Attentive posture and position, ie, not too close, but not too distant; leaning forward, but not aggressively.

Here are some of the variances you might encounter in the way people speak:

Speech dimension	Characteristics
Volume	Loudness, quietness, audibility.
Stress	Modulated, unmodulated.
Tone	Admiring, disparaging.
Clarity	Clear enunciation, mumbling, slurring.
Pace	Fast, slow, how easy it is to follow.

These variances might mean a number of things; for example, a drop to a very quiet voice might signify a shyness about that particular subject. Some people have naturally monotonous voices, so don't read too much into it! A great deal of the emotional content of what is being said will be conveyed by vocal characteristics. 'He's a great help' might be either admiring or disparaging, depending on the way it is said.

Try saying,   He's a great help.

He's a great help.

He's a great help   in different tones and expressions....

Body communication	Characteristics
Proximity	Closeness, distance.
Posture orientation	Facing, turning away, forwards, backwards.
Posture	Tense, relaxed, rigid, slouched.
Facial expression	Animated, blank.
Eye contact	Staring, darting about, avoiding eye contact, seeking eye contact.
Gesture	Amount, variety, animated, helpless, aggressive.

You need to be careful not to misinterpret non-verbal communication. The client sitting very stiffly may have a bad back: they may not be defensively touching their nose; they may be about to sneeze! It is important to learn to interpret the behaviours; for example:

- Why are they avoiding eye contact?
- Is the subject matter threatening?
- Why are they leaning back in their chair?
- Are they bored, or distancing themselves from the question?

It is also important to match the body language to the words being spoken. For example, 'I am very happy in my job' spoken through clenched teeth with hands fidgeting is an 'incongruent' statement, ie, the non verbal behaviour does not match the words. However, if you can perceive messages accurately, you are in a much more powerful position to understand clients. (If in doubt, observe for longer, to see if it is a repeating pattern. Beware over-zealousness!)

Here are some obstacles to effective listening, and some suggestions for improving listening.

Self consciousness

If the listener is preoccupied with themselves, or is over-concerned about the image they are creating listening is likely to suffer.

Remember that you are not performing. It is the speaker who is your main concern. Anything that distracts you from what the speaker is saying, will destroy the communication.

Concentrate on the speaker, not yourself

Daydreaming

The listener may get lost in their own thoughts and memories, and the interaction gets lost.

Concentrate! You can usually direct your attention where you wish. Effective listeners offer full and total concentration on the speaker. Recognise why you are daydreaming.

Emotional messages

The content of what the speaker is saying may arouse anger or hostility in the listener. The resulting emotions may block listening, or cause a distortion of the message.

Be aware of your own feelings, and the reasons why the message content is so emotional for you. This will enable you to try to counteract the distortion to your understanding.

The long speech

The listener forgets the middle parts of long speeches, or loses track of the logic.

Don't be afraid to ask if you feel you are losing the thread. It is useful to summarise what you think you have heard, and check that you have got it right so far. Ask for clarification if you are still confused.

The boring repetitive speech

The listener gets bored with what the speaker has to say, particularly as they seem to be repeating themselves.

Why are they repeating themselves? Is it because you have not heard them? You may need to tell them that they have already said that, but beware, in case you haven't heard exactly what they are saying. Check it out.

Reductive listening

The listener may modify the message received so that it sounds like previous messages. You tend to assume that people don't change.

Don't make assumptions about what is being, or what you think is going to be said. People are not consistent. They may change, or say things which seem inconsistent to you. Ask the speaker to clarify.

Hearing what you want to hear

Your own motives and expectations lead you to assume that others share same view. It may even lead you to premature conclusions, and 'rigged evidence'.

Make a conscious effort to be aware of your motives and expectations. If the speaker only says what you would have expected them to say, then you have learned nothing from the conversation. Avoid premature conclusions about the client's problems.

'You agree with me'

The listener may modify what is heard to fit in with their own attitudes or opinions, screening out contrary information.

Don't be afraid to explore new or different perspectives. Having different ideas does not always lead to hostility or conflict – sometimes quite the reverse.

'You disagree with me'

The opposite also happens: that a listener feels hostility or infers that what is being said is against their own views.

Think about your feelings for the speaker, and try to distinguish them from your feelings about the message. Concentrate on the content of the message.

Evaluation

You tend to evaluate messages in terms of 'good/bad', 'right/wrong', etc. This clouds communication and if evaluation is negative, may turn off the speaker

It doesn't matter what your opinion is. Your role is to listen to the speaker, not to put your personal viewpoint across. Try not to evaluate, and focus on the speaker's right to their own views.

Rehearsing a reply

Part of the way through the message, the listener may start preparing a response, or another question, and become preoccupied. This will lose the message.

As soon as you want to start speaking you are less effective as a listener. If you want the speaker to continue, stop rehearsing. You can give yourself time to respond after they have finished.

Environmental noise

External distractions can prevent the message getting through.

Try to prevent distractions before they happen. If one does occur, remove it, or if this is not possible, reschedule or change location.

Having looked at enabling the client to '*tell the story*', we need to look at ways of *exploring and understanding the situation*.

■ Stage Two: Understanding the situation

The counsellor helps the client to piece together the picture that has emerged in Stage One. They help them see broader issues and patterns where relevant, and so develop new perspectives on themselves and their situation. It also increases an awareness of the need for action.

In order to understand the situation, the counsellor needs:

- The skills of Stage One.
- Confrontation.
- Analysis.
- Timing and pacing.
- Lateral thinking.
- Offering new perspectives.

At this stage, the counsellor needs all the skills of Stage One. *You don't ever stop listening or observing in a counselling session.* You are continuing to observe and listen, but are now ready to take the process a stage further.

The client is starting to talk, and by now you should be getting a good idea of what the situation is. It may not be the one you thought it would be. It may not be the situation the client thought it would be. Frequently, someone will be referred to you for what appears to be a valid reason. Don't try and deal with that reason until you have established whether it is the true issue.

For example, Jonathan came to see his manager because he felt that his time management was poor, and he wanted to go on a course. The 'presenting problem' was Jonathan's 'poor' time management. On discussing the matter further, it appeared that Jonathan had plenty of time to do the tasks he was supposed to do. However, he was not sure how to do them, and no-one had shown him how. Therefore the real problem was not one of time management, but a question of assessing Jonathan's skills, and their relation to the job he was supposed to be doing. Problems often arise when counsellors get lost in the detail of the story, and in doing so, lose both the message and the person.

So what do you need to look for, when you are listening to a person's story? What you need is a **DRAWING** of the person:

D Description of self: Clients are not aware of how they describe themselves. They frequently use recurring themes, words and phrases in their 'stories', for example, conflict. It is these scenarios that give the counsellor an insight into the client's self perception.

R Role: How do people view themselves when they tell you their story? Are they active or passive? Do they seek or take responsibility? Do they see everything as happening to them? Do they accept blame, or do they consistently put the blame outside of themselves?

A Attitude: What kind of feelings do they have about the difficulty they are facing? Are they hopeful or despairing? Do they feel betrayed, lost or do they have some central reserve of confidence that they can build on to comfort themselves with?

W The **Way the story is told**: This is a key element of counselling; the tone in which the story is told is the most significant source of insight for the counsellor. The client might be describing a trivial or important incident, but how are they relaying it? Are they telling it in a depressed, tired, 'don't care' way? Is there anger bubbling behind their words? Is there a feeling of a loss or gain of power behind this simple story? Why have they chosen this particular story? The counsellor's response should be not to the details of the story, but to the underlying tone which gives the story its meaning.

I Interested parties: Who is involved in the story? Are there recurring characters, or characters with similar behaviours and effects? How do they relate to the client? How does the client feel about them?

N Nature of the conflict: What is the nature of the conflict? How does it show itself? Is it a recurring conflict in other situations, in or out of work? What is at the heart of the conflict?

G Going over it: Have you heard this story before? Were you listening before, or is the client trying to underline a point? It may not be the same story in its details, but are the theme and conflict the same? Clients repeat stories because they feel the counsellor hasn't heard, or is not giving enough emphasis to the particular point they are trying to make.

10·Dealing with Disruptive Processes

■ Summary

An important part of Stage Two, 'Understanding the Problem', is the ability to recognise when a client needs to be brought face to face with some issues that they have been avoiding. Without the counsellor doing this, the client will be unable to move on.

It means being able to recognise and understand defences, and being able to point them out without destroying them. It means confronting and feeding back descriptions of behaviour. It is also necessary to challenge the games clients use to avoid dealing with issues, both wittingly and unwittingly. Once you are dealing with the real issues you can begin to analyse them and look at their implications before moving on to the next stage. A good counsellor needs to be aware of situations where confrontation is called for, skilled in the skills of confrontation, and assertive enough to use them.

Confronting literally means bringing someone face to face with what is happening, and what they are doing. This involves accurate, objective and specific descriptions of what is happening.

■ Dealing with distractions

Sometimes at this stage of the interview, you may feel that the drawing does not quite fit together. It may be helpful to ask yourself, 'I could move the client on, if I understood...'. When you can finish the sentence, you can progress the client on. It is breaking down what the blocks to understanding are, that is crucial to getting the story straight, and identify the true issues, not just the 'presenting' ones. Only then can you help the client to deal with the issues. At this stage, a sense of timing is crucial. If you interrupt the client, you may prevent them telling the story in the terms they want to use. If you wait too long to respond, the client may perceive you as passive or disinterested. There is a rhythm to telling and understanding the story, which allows for the counsellor's intervention. Clients almost always provide the necessary breaks to do this. You, as a counsellor, have to listen for them.

Sometimes, when you or the client are facing an issue which is uncomfortable, or you feel you might be put in a position where you feel vulnerable, your first reaction will be to avoid it. This is done in many subtle ways, but the basic aim is always the same; avoid the potentially threatening issue. Frequently, people do not know they are doing this; it may be an instinctive defensive reaction.

■ Why do people have and use defences?

Through the processes of growing and trying out different experiences, each individual develops a set of ideas about themselves. They will have an idea about the sort of person they are, in each of their social roles: as a parent; as a spouse; as a manager; as a team player, etc. They will also have an ideal view of themselves; of the sort of person they feel they ought, or would like, to be. This ideal view also covers their values, dreams and fantasies about themselves and their place in society.

■ The self concept

This set of ideas is known collectively as the '*self concept*'. One definition of being 'emotionally mature' is the process of developing a realistic self concept. This is one in which the person's view of themselves is largely in agreement with other people's view of them. Many emotional and psychological problems have their roots in an unrealistic or inappropriate self concept.

The individual is likely to be quite open in discussing some aspects of the self concept. For example, when someone says, 'I've never thought of myself as the sporty type' or 'I've never thought of myself as quite an approachable person'.

However, other aspects of the self concept will be totally private. In fact, they are the most private of all possessions (the very top of the communications pyramid). These aspects, which are likely to be of central importance, are never discussed, even with those close to them, and certainly not with work colleagues. Individuals guard the concept of themselves most carefully of all, because the self concept is them.

■ Defence mechanisms

The individual develops a range of devices with which to guard themselves from criticism. These are defence mechanisms.

Typical defences include:

- Denial, or rejection of information.
  For example, 'That's just not true. I'm never like that.'
- Blaming others, 'circumstances beyond our control' or the weather.
  For example, 'It wasn't my fault. They all left me with it.'
- Lying.
  For example, 'He never gave me any information about it.'
- Agreeing quickly.
  For example, 'Oh, that's absolutely right. I'll try it your way tomorrow.'
- Changing the subject.
  For example, 'Well, it's not getting the contract that's important. It's the fact that I wasn't told about the change of plan.'

There are many more, and some come in a combination. There is no one reason people use particular mechanisms at particular times. It seems that each person discovers and then develops those defences which work for them personally, in different situations.

In some cultures, feedback is relatively easily accepted. For example, in Australia, it is not unusual for strangers or slight acquaintances to make personal comments. In a culture of privacy, like Britain, feedback is rarely given, and even praise is received defensively. 'Oh, it was nothing really. Anyone could have done it.' Feedback creates an awareness of the need for change. This implies, particularly to the British, that the individual is somehow inadequate for failing to spot the need themselves. This leads to a feeling of guilt, and then to defensiveness.

It is very difficult to know how central a particular piece of behaviour is to a person's self concept. Apparently trivial behaviours can represent key themes. For example, a scruffy appearance may simply reflect that you did not know they minded about it, or it may imply a deep seated concern to be seen as creative, individual and independent. A constant 'devil may care' attitude may indicate a very deep concern to do the 'right' thing. *If a behaviour is important, it is likely to be highly defended.*

The pattern of defence that people use is not accidental, neither is it just throwing up obstacles to keep the counsellor at bay. The style of the defence will tell you a great deal about the client. (The style of your response will tell you a great deal about you...). It is an insightful and descriptive language that counsellors need to translate and understand, rather that try to get rid of it in an irritated way. Counselling is not a situation in which the counsellor can 'win'. When it feels like that, it means that you are as defensive as the client, and must prove yourself by 'conquering' the client.

The counsellor needs to evaluate the client's defence mechanisms, before dealing with them:

- How long have they been there?
- What happened to challenge the defence mechanisms, and bring them up at this stage?
- How much does this person need them in order to function 'normally' at this moment in time?
- If the defences are not working as well as they have done in the past, why is this?
- Is this a sign that their ability to cope is lessening, or are they getting closer to an important insight into themselves?
- What kind of defences do people use?

Intellectualisation

This defence is about being able to think about the problems in an abstract way, and talk about them theoretically. Somehow, this keeps the problem 'out there' rather then within the person. In this way clients need feel no emotion, and can talk on and on. They often use psychological terminology, and while it may sound as though the client is talking about significant subjects, they are avoiding themselves, which is the main issue.

You will probably have to point out to the client the way they are using this defence. You do *not* do this by saying, 'Do you realise that you are using an intellectual defence to avoid telling the truth about yourself?' This is answering the client in kind. A more appropriate response would be one that reflected the counsellor's own state of mind, at that moment in the relationship. This is usually a feeling of being kept on the outside, or at arm's length from the client. So you might say, 'We seem to be talking a lot, but don't appear to be getting very far.' Or, 'I understand what you are saying, but I don't get any feeling of you being involved in the situation.'

Expressing irritation

When a counsellor gets a little too close to the source of the problem, clients frequently respond by getting irritable. This can deflect the counsellor by getting *them* angry, thus throwing them off the scent of the client's issues. It is essential that the counsellor responds to the person rather than to the defensive attack. 'It sounds as though this is a difficult subject for you to discuss,' might be the kind of response that would be appropriate in this case. This is taking the conversation back to the client, and away from the counsellor.

Diverting

Another method of avoiding an issue is to either change or divert the subject, or launch into irrelevant detail that confuses the counsellor. The only thing to do here is to bring the client back, by using phrases like: 'That's certainly true. I feel that we are getting away from the point. Can we just go back to...'.

In order to get past the defences to deal with the real issues, the counsellor will have to confront the client. Confrontation is not a heavy stick to beat people with. The counsellor needs to understand why they are confronting, and are not using it as a way of showing up other people's weaknesses, and thereby their own superiority. Confrontation is used to point out the defences, not destroy them. It is very easy to feel hostile towards a client who is provoking you, or leading you off the track. It is sometimes even satisfying to respond in a hostile way. However, a hostile response means that you are no longer counselling. You have entered into a 'game' with the client, and your responding in this way will ensure their control. This is neither confrontation, nor is it constructive.

Sometimes the 'gameplaying' is actually the problem itself. This 'gameplaying' is usually started by the client (although not always). If the counsellor does not recognise it and deal with it, there will be no constructive result to the discussion. There will be many times when the counsellor is drawn in to the 'game', for many reasons. This is called '*colluding*'. In order to stop the 'game', the counsellor will have to confront the client. *Confronting does not mean aggression.*

■ Playing games

If people become comfortable with their delusions they will try to hang on to them. They may get their satisfaction by playing games in the interview, or outside the interview. Eric Berne's theory of transactional analysis suggested that if people got what they wanted from playing games, they would obviously continue to play them. He suggested that people often wrote themselves 'scripts'. Like a play, these are a series of actions and sentences which form a familiar response system for them. These scripts are patterns of behaviour that affect the way people act in their personal life, and what they do and say on the job. They may follow patterns, such as always fumbling, never quite making it, getting to the top, getting put down, getting things their way, putting others down, always striving, etc.

People get used to reacting in a particular way, and sometimes it may be part of the counsellor's role to point this out to the client. The number of games people can play to avoid dealing with life is endless. Here are some descriptions of the games most commonly found in organisational settings.

Sometimes the initiator of the game will set up or observe a situation where somebody makes a mistake, only to step in at a later stage to triumphantly point out the error. They are doing this to give themselves a feeling of superiority and, by putting someone else down, they feel good about themselves, ie, more powerful.

There is a game where the player, by constantly misunderstanding directives or information, convinces themselves of their own lack of intelligence. This game is clearly recognised, for they are the people who constantly misunderstand when everyone else understands most clearly. These people do not want to feel powerful and good about themselves; quite the reverse. They want to feel 'not OK', and use this game to avoid facing up to themselves. At some stage in the game they are likely to actually say 'I must be stupid'. Their aim is to make you say that they are.

Another way the initiator might make themselves feel 'OK' about themselves is to ask for solutions to a problem they pose. As each solution is prefaced by the remark 'Why don't you...?', the game player is always able to counter with the argument 'Yes, but...', followed by a rejection of the idea. The more you try to offer ideas, the more powerful they feel, and the more frustrated you feel. This game is frequently played at meetings and counselling sessions. (And is yet another good reason for not telling the client what to do...)

If these games are a way of avoiding dealing with life, then it is important that the counsellor challenges them by feeding back to the client what they are doing. The feedback should be given in a way that the client will accept! For example, they are unlikely to accept derogatory words like, 'You're manipulative' or 'That's being selfish'. If you want to tell the client that they are being manipulative, you have to describe the behaviours involved, without judging them. A value judgement would immediately invite either a denial, or a game from the client.

This means that you need to *describe the situation and behaviours in a specific way*. If, for example, you wanted to tell a client that you felt that they were selfish, you must describe the kind of things the client has done to lead you to this conclusion. For example, 'You have mentioned on several occasions that when people are discussing things you are not interested in, you switch off. You have described your impatience with members of staff who do not understand what you say the first time you say it.' These are descriptions of the person's behaviour.

It also helps to describe what happens as a result of their behaviour. For example, how other people are affected by their behaviour:

Counsellor What do you think you do that upsets the team?
Client Well, I do demand a very high standard of neatness in their work, and I can't abide sloppy dressers. I always tell them, as soon as they walk in the door.

The purpose of giving the feedback is to show the client what they are doing, and understand its impact on others. Confrontation is not meant to be a personal exchange. It does not end with the counsellor identifying or exposing the defence or defensive behaviour of the client. **Confronting literally means bringing someone face to face with what is happening and what they are doing . This involves accurate, objective and specific descriptions of what is happening.** This step is the beginning of working with the real issues, as opposed to the presenting problem.

11· *Moving On*

■ Summary

This is potentially the most challenging stage in the interview process, and the one where the counsellor is most active. It is also the one which will be seen as having the most importance to the organisation, as it is about results. The counsellor needs to identify and agree on a course of action for the client, and help them plan ways of implementing it. They also need to look at some of the issues that can stop the client achieving their goals.
The counsellor needs the skills of:

- Analysis and problem solving.
- Feedback.
- A knowledge of resources.
- Goal setting.
- Helping clients assess strategies and choose appropriately.
- Helping the client draw up realistic plans.
- Supporting and maintaining the client through implementation.

This is the third stage in the counselling process. Having got the story, and explored and understood the situation, you are ready to move in to the final stage:

Moving on   developing strategies, gaining acceptance.

The counsellor aims to help the client to act, based on their new understanding of themselves and their situation. The client and counsellor agree on a course of action. The counsellor explores with the client a variety of ways of achieving the goals that have been set, and helps them identify what resources and strengths they have and can use. They help the client choose and work out for themselves a specific plan of action, taking into account costs to themselves and others. The counsellor supports them in implementing their plan, and helps them evaluate the results.

In order to move on, the counsellor needs :

- All the skills of Stages One and Two.
- Goal setting.
- To use creative thinking and problem solving techniques.
- To encourage and support.
- A knowledge of resources.
- A knowledge of how behaviour is changed and maintained.

The counsellor is most active, in terms of their input, in this stage. However, the fundamental principle of letting the client solve their own problem is still paramount.

In terms of the organisation, this is the most important stage: the action stage. The manager as counsellor is balancing on the fence between their client's needs and the organisation's needs. The organisation may not be able to give the client the time to pace or direct themselves.

The counsellor's experience at Stage Three may be greater than the client's, and the skill of this stage is one of imparting the knowledge without telling the client what to do. The first thing the counsellor and client must agree is the direction that the client needs to take: which *goals* to aim for.

■ Goal setting

Everything in Stages One and Two is preparatory to this:

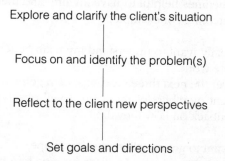

Goal setting completes the process. Everything done after the goal process, for example, choosing strategies and implementing action plans, is done to ensure that the goals are met. The real challenge of counselling for some does not lie in the identification of problem situations: it is frequently found in the *management* of these situations. Sometimes clients (and counsellors!) want to skip the goal setting process once they have identified the problem. They just want to deal with it immediately. Sometimes, the converse is true: problems can make the client feel shut off and overwhelmed.

A goal helps to keep the client (and the counsellor) achievement-oriented. It helps them to picture themselves managing the situation.

Clear goals:

- Focus the client's attention on action.
- Motivate the client to look for strategies.
- Give clients a reason to persevere.

■ Guidelines for goal setting

S   **Specific**

M   **Measurable**

A   **Activity and achievement based**

R   **Realistic**

T   **Timed**

Smart people know exactly what they are trying to achieve.

Specific

Vague goals allow you to put them off, for example, 'My New Year resolution is to get in shape this year.' Vague aims are wishes rather than goals.

A goal is a statement of what you want to do, and how you want to do it.

It is sometimes helpful to have an aim, and then translate the aim into a specific outcome. For example:

AIM: 'I really want to understand my team better, and be able to delegate more work.'

GOAL: 'Over the next three meetings, I am going to delegate the chair to different members of the team. I will observe, discuss and give them feedback on how they did.'

AIM: 'I want to get myself in physical shape.'

GOAL: 'Within six months, I will be running four miles in under 50 minutes, at least three times a week.'

In both these cases, a particular behaviour is being described. In the latter, a pattern is established and consistently pursued.

Measurable

You must be able to tell whether you have achieved your goal or not. Without this knowledge, you feel no accomplishment. You cannot know if you are making progress, if you don't know where you started. For example,

'I want to cut out time wasting in meetings,' is not measurable;
'By the end of the month, I will have had two meetings, lasting no longer than two hours each.'

It is not always necessary to put numbers in to measure progress, but some quantifier is necessary.

Activity and achievement based

The achievements of the goals are not the way to get there. They are what will have been accomplished or achieved at the end. For example, 'I need to get some training in interpersonal skills' is a method rather than an achievement. The goal is only achieved when you have gained, practised and actually used those skills in interpersonal situations.

Gerard Egan suggests using the 'past participle' approach; for example, skills *acquired*, drinking *stopped*, number of meetings *decreased*. It is about knowing what you want from the method, as an outcome, rather than what the method consists of, ie, what you want to get at the end of it.

Realistic

A goal is realistic if:

- The client has the resources necessary to achieve the goal.
- There are no external circumstances preventing them achieving the goal.
- The cost of achieving it is not too high.

> 'Nothing breeds success like success. Conversely, nothing causes feelings of despair like personal failure. A primary principle of goal setting is to measure the motivation level of the individual. But goal setting can have precisely the opposite effect if it produces a yardstick that constantly makes the individual feel inadequate.'[1]

Clients can sabotage their efforts if they choose goals that are beyond their reach, or which include resources that are beyond their control. For example, Steven wants to move into the training department of his organisation. However, there are no vacancies at present, and the department is, in fact, shedding staff. Therefore it would not be a good idea for Steven to set a goal that involved moving into the training department, as he will be unable to influence its result.

It is also important that the goals are the client's goals, and not the counsellor's. Carl Rogers, in a film of a counselling session,[2] is asked by a client what she should do about her relationship with her daughter. He says: 'I think you have been telling me all along what you want to do.' The client actually knew what she wanted to do; what she wanted from the counsellor was not his suggestions, but his *approval* for what she wanted to do. If he had given her his approval, the goal would have become his goal, instead of hers. At another point in the interview he asks: 'What is it that you want me to tell you to do?' This puts the responsibility for the goal setting back where it belongs; with the client.

Timed

Like vague and non-specific goals, those that are to be done 'sometime or other', or with no time frame, never seem to get done. If an individual says, 'I am going to set aside three hours a week to organise my staff group, as soon as this current rush is over', they are unlikely to achieve the goal, because the time frame is not clear. It is almost like paying 'lip service' to the idea of a goal, without ever really intending to achieve it.

For a goal to be achieved, it must meet all of the SMART rules. If any one component is missing, it could be the element that stops the person dealing with the problem. Having defined the goals, you can move on to identifying how to attain them. There are three stages to this process:

- Identifying and assessing strategies.
- Helping clients put together a plan of action.
- Helping clients to implement the plans.

Strategy is the art of identifying and choosing realistic methods of achieving goals. It also means looking at ways of getting round problems that may arise. What sort of issues prevent people from solving problems?

- Reliance *on authority giving them the answers*. People come to the counsellor expecting the right answer, and may sometimes block efforts to help them by playing games like 'Yes but...'
- *Fear.* Clients are often fearful of suggesting ideas that might sound stupid, and their anxiety about the problem gets in the way of them dealing with it.
- *Long term habits.* Some clients have deeply ingrained behaviour patterns, and as such are resistant to change.
- *Long stay problem.* The problem has been around a long time, and the client still has no idea of how to deal with it.

There are a number of ways the counsellor can help the client break the block that is stopping them developing strategies. Some of the problems arise because it is very easy to get caught in the trap of only seeing things in one dimension: for example, if you were shown a rubber tyre, and asked how many uses you could find for it, your initial thoughts would be centred around what you know to be the 'normal' uses of a tyre, ie, put it on a car. Your list would be very short, and then you would become 'blocked'. This is because if you only view things in one light, you tend to evaluate any problems associated with it in the same one light. Your mind screens off anything outside of that dimension. The kind of thinking that makes you think like this is called 'convergent thinking'. It partly stems from school, where you are encouraged to give only 'right' answers ('wrong' or creative answers are not rewarded, and are usually ignored or punished) and therefore learn to evaluate everything before saying anything.

However, many problems in life are too complex for 'convergent' thinking, and you need more perspectives. This is known as 'divergent' thinking. But it is difficult to do this, because you are so programmed to think in a straight line.

■ Brainstorming

One way of getting round this is to use a technique called 'brainstorming'. Brainstorming is a technique for generating ideas, possibilities and alternative courses of action. The objective is to identify as many ideas as possible. When you brainstorm, you write down anything you think of, without evaluating it first. That means you write it down, however silly it sounds. So if you go back to the tyre example, you could find yourself writing things like 'hula hoop, necklace, boat...'. Some of these suggestions are silly, but don't evaluate them until you have got as many thoughts as you can in five minutes.

If you use this technique when you are trying to help clients identify possible strategies for achieving goals, it is very important that they do not criticise the ideas they are generating, at the initial stages. Suspending judgement in this way also helps avoid the client playing 'Yes, but...'. So don't say things like 'Explain what you mean', or 'I'm not sure I like that idea'. Even the craziest possibilities may have the kernel of an idea in them. The more ideas they develop, the more likelihood there is of finding one that will work. When you have all the ideas, then it helps for the counsellor to clarify some, before evaluating for example,

Client I suppose there might be the possibility of a transfer.
Counsellor Are there different types of transfer available at the moment?

This is still leaving the problem with the client, but helping them to clarify ideas often leads to new possibilities. After this process, you can begin to evaluate the ideas you have in relation to the problem, and the resources the client has. (Skills, knowledge, emotional resources). It is helpful to analyse potential strategies in terms of potential benefits and potential losses, and the acceptability or unacceptability of the benefits or losses.

Some strategies are quite simple and their achievement method is very obvious. Others are more complicated and demand the client working out a step by step procedure for achieving their goals. When helping the client formulate a plan of action, it is useful to use the same guidelines as those for goal setting. When they formulate their action plans, they often come up against some of the problems they will face in implementing them. It is part of the counsellor's role to help the client deal with the obstacles, and not avoid them or be deterred from carrying on. Many clients will, however, make decisions based on impulse and bias, rather than a logical thought procedure. It is important for the counsellor to remind themselves of their non-directive role, ie, it is the client's decision, and while you can point out various issues, at the end of the day, you cannot *make* them do anything.

Some clients have a clear idea of what they are going to do, and are ready to walk out of the session at this point: all they want to do is get started. Others may need support and maintenance to implement their plans. If their plan fails, or comes to a halt, or the client becomes overcome by inertia, it may fall to the counsellor to facilitate the client.

■ Results in the workplace

Helping the client to implement their plans is a part of the counselling role that is often forgotten, because in many professional counselling cases, a plan might not be appropriate. However, it is particularly relevant to managers counselling internally. This is because it is about *results in the workplace.*

When a plan does not work or falls apart, it is helpful to be able to understand and analyse what has made it do so. Kurt Lewin, in his forcefield theory, said that there were two forces to analyse when problem solving: those that stop you from achieving your goals, and those that help you. It is also useful for the counsellor to give the client feedback about how they have perceived them implementing their plans. Again, this particularly applies to counselling in the workplace, and it is part of the manager's role to observe a client's progress. (It might be important to build in this 'monitoring' dimension into the contract.)

For example, Alan Brown was a very bright, articulate, capable manager. He had a reputation for very high quality work, almost to the point of obsession. He had just taken over the role of team manager in an Information Technology department of a large company. He had a team of committed individuals, who were technically good, and always brought projects in on time, but only just. Alan was feeling very overloaded by the amount of work and the time pressures he felt under. He respected and admired his manager but felt he was getting little support from him although the manager relied heavily on Alan. He was completely exhausted trying to do everything, and was beginning to be very short tempered with his staff. His manager eventually called him in to his office, and they came to the conclusion that Alan wasn't delegating enough of his work, and had taken on a role that was inappropriate. Together they put together some goals and an action plan to enable Alan to 'let go' of some of his jobs, and use his time more efficiently. Alan went away, initially satisfied, but when it came to implementing his plan, he found it difficult to put in any of his new structure, as his boss kept giving him new projects, and appeared to have forgotten their discussion. They met again, and Alan and his boss tried to analyse what was stopping him from achieving his goals.

They analysed the situation as follows:

Things that were stopping Alan achieve his goals	Things that were helping Alan achieve his goals
His manager was continually giving him work, when he already had far too much.	His manager was genuinely concerned for Alan, and respected his skills and abilities.
Alan did not feel his work was valued by his manager, and therefore he was tentative about instigating new procedures.	His manager wanted the same final achievement as Alan.
Alan's manager was not quite sure of his role, and therefore was interfering with Alan.	Alan was very highly motivated to put in new structures, in order delegate appropriately, and free his time.
	The team were very supportive of Alan, and endorsed his plans for reorganisation.

Once they had analysed it in this way, it was very easy to work on the issues that were preventing him using some of the things that were helping him. So, for example, they sorted out the misunderstandings that were occurring between Alan and his manager.

Some people may baulk at the idea of the mechanistic approach to goal setting and problem solving: it may not be appropriate for all clients. Like all the techniques we have described in this book, it is an approach to be considered and adapted to the situation, rather than rigidly followed.

■ Ending the session

Having established a plan of action with the client, it is time for you to end the session. Many inexperienced counsellors underestimate the importance of ending a session professionally. If the ending does not refer back to the initial contract, it will be difficult to see what has been achieved. If there is no explicit end to the interview, the client (and the counsellor) can feel uncomfortable.

If you have set your contract at the beginning of the session, it is easy to terminate when you agreed to. Most experienced counsellors restrict time for various reasons:

- Needing to be on time for other appointments.
- Training clients to understand limits of time, so that they can use the time in the session to full effect.

- Putting a very tangible end to the process makes it more 'secure' for the client.
- It prevents a professional contact becoming a personal one.

However, there may be emergencies which justify the occasional deviation from ending on time. Professional counsellors pace their session so that things are leading up to the end. When you are counselling as a manager, it is more likely that when the time you have set is nearly up, you will have to summarise, and say something like, 'Well, we have about five minutes to go...' and maybe add a tentative question, if appropriate, 'I'm wondering whether there is anything further you would like to bring up before we finish.'

When starting out counselling, some counsellors are not assertive enough when finishing off their sessions. Sometimes they let them drift on, or finish the session in such a way that the client perceives it as a lack of interest. It is quite helpful to refer back to the contract, and the agreed perceived outcomes and expectations. This helps to give a structured, 'rounded-off', feel to both the client and counsellor, about where you have come from, and what you have achieved. In that light, it is also useful to sum up the action points, and do a final check back. For example, 'So we have agreed that you will keep a log of all your activities this week. We will meet again next Tuesday at three o'clock, for an hour, when we will analyse the implications of your log in terms of you managing your time, and delegating more tasks. Is that OK?'

■ Note-keeping

One more issue which needs to be addressed is the issue of keeping notes and records. Some counsellors take copious notes through the sessions. Others make notes at the end of the interview. Some do not take notes at all. The normal reason people give for taking notes is that they might forget things that are said.

It is important to establish the purpose of the notes: are they for the counsellor or the client? What will happen to them at the end of the session? Are they to establish progress against goals set? Are they for analysis, to help plan other ways of thinking?

If you listen and summarise carefully, you will not forget things because you will be constantly updating the flow. Of course, you might miss the odd word, but that needs to be balanced against the effect notetaking has on the interview:

- It disturbs the flow because you lose eye contact.
- It can be threatening to the client because they cannot see what you are writing. This will affect their willingness to speak.
- It distracts the client, and may make them (and/or the counsellor) lose their train of thought.

Bearing these points in mind, can your note-taking wait, or is it necessary? What will you do with the notes? Will the client feel happy with a written record, however note-formed? How does it affect confidentiality? You need to consider these questions before making a decision. If you do decide to take notes, ensure that you tell the client, and explain your reasons and what will happen to the notes in order to reassure him of your motives.

■ References

1. Locke, E.A. and Latham, G.P., *Goal Setting: a Motivational Technique That Works*, Prentice Hall, 1984

12·*Your Feelings as a Counsellor*

■ Summary

The counsellor stands to learn and develop almost as much as the client during the counselling process. They can only do this, and deal appropriately with the client, if they are aware of the issues that affect the counsellor. The two major threats to the counsellor come from insufficient self awareness, and confusing their own personal issues with those of the client. If the counsellor is not aware of their own feelings, they will find it difficult to be objective with a client, and distinguish their own feelings from the client's. Not only do you have to concentrate on, and listen to the client, you have to know yourself.

Points to take note of are:

- Insufficient self awareness.
- Threats to self esteem.
- Limits of ability.
- Personal attacks.
- Confusing personal issues with client's.
- Identifying with the client.
- Projection.
- Transference.
- Letting go.
- Dealing with the client's emotional dependency.
- Conquering personal dependency.

Counselling tools:

- Know yourself and your reactions.
- Listen to the client.
- Concentrate on the person, not the problem.
- Don't rescue.
- Respond to the person instead of trying to make a good response.

────────

'*The more you understand people, the more you understand yourself.*
The more you understand yourself, the more you understand people.'

If effective interpersonal helping is always tied to the relationship with the other person, then you must focus on yourself, as you are when you are with that person. You often think that if you get enough information about the other person, this is enough. This is crucial to understanding their situation, but you also have to take into consideration yourself and your own reactions. This is the demanding double focus that is essential for counselling.

You must know what is taking place inside yourself as well as inside others. These feelings are sometimes interrelated. The potential stress of un-recognised and unmanaged personal involvement is very strong. As a coun-sellor, you have to know who you are, and why you react in the way you do. Those who do not understand themselves, or what is happening in the course of the process, can easily get lost. This is not because the client has such complex problems, but because the counsellor has not learned to take their own situation into account.

So there are two issues:

- Not being able to deal with the problem, because your personal issues prevent you and you don't know it.
- Not being able to deal with the problem, and not knowing why.

So it is better to understand some of the issues or dynamics of the 'helping' situation. To remain empathic (remember empathy? Understanding what someone is saying and its implications) demands both a sense of yourself and a sense of the client. It begins with the very base line of listening to the client. This is not the same as waiting for another person to finish before you start talking. Nor does it mean daydreaming while someone tells what you consider to be a very familiar story. It means giving up your own thoughts and interests for a while, in order to be able to give your complete attention to the other person. They tell you *that* something is going on, and they give you major clues as to *what* is going on. Listening for, and interpre-ting these clues provides you with the answer to whether you will be able to be of any help to the client.

These considerations lead to the questions of some of the feelings you experience as a counsellor, and the effect they have on both your reactions, and those of the client.

Try to ignore the use of jargon, and concentrate on understanding ideas that are not complicated, but extremely important. They describe some of the processes that go on in the enabling or empowering relationship.

■ The client's feelings

Let us first look at those feelings the person you are helping seems to have towards you in the counselling relationship. They are feelings which are ap-propriate to previous significant figures in their lives. This could include parents, or those who took their place. These feelings are present all the time, but they are more pronounced in the counselling relationship. In a professional counselling situation, this is a very important stage of the pro-cess. In terms of counselling in the workplace, it may manifest itself in a more dilute form: this might mean that feelings towards the organisation or bosses might be shown in the client's behaviour towards you in the inter-view. These feelings could be either positive or negative. Counsellors should be aware that this can happen. They should not feel that the person feels this way towards them as individuals.

For example, if the individual has had a promotion knocked by company restructuring, and is feeling very anti-company, they may express their anger at the counsellor, because it is a channel that has presented itself. If the counsellor takes this personally, they are not listening to what the client is saying. They are not angry with *you*, and the problem is not *you*. The problem is with the client's feelings towards the organisation. It is this issue that you have to deal with. These feelings are a dilute form of what is called, in a therapeutic counselling process, *transference*.

■ The counsellor's feelings

The other side of this part of the process are the feelings you have for the individual who you are counselling. These feelings may include feelings of being strongly attracted to, or unattracted to the person. There is nothing wrong with having these feelings about people. A problem only arises when you avoid acknowledging the feelings, because they arouse in you feelings of surprise, shame or guilt. You have to identify these feelings, in order to understand and help your client.

These feelings are similar to the process of *countertransference* in the therapeutic counselling process. For example, a male manager might find himself attracted to a female member of staff he is interviewing. Defensive about himself, he does not admit these reactions and only expresses them indirectly. He treats the woman harshly, and antagonises her frequently. This is not because of anything she has said or done, but in response to his own unconscious feelings of attraction to her. He has established distance from her in a destructive way, in order to handle his own feelings. The irony of the situation is that although he does not acknowledge these feelings, they dominate the relationship anyway, and prevent him understanding the client.

At this point, it might be helpful to list a few '**DO NOTS**':

DO NOT PANIC   The calmer you are, the more likely you are to hear the signals coming from your client, as well as from yourself. The key to this is getting patience and a willingness to suspend action, until you have a fairly good idea of the sources and nature of their reaction and your own.

DO NOT MISINTERPRET   Try not to leap in, which is the easiest thing to do in a situation where you feel out of control. This generally makes things worse for both you and the client. It is worth mentally sitting back and letting things become clear to the client. If you listen carefully, the meaning will become clearer.

(If you feel that is too simplistic, try it. It is astonishing how the quality of listening and hearing can enlarge your vision of a situation.)

DO NOT FORCE REACTIONS   Do not try to artificially change either your reactions or those of the client. Instead of covering emotional tracks, you should learn from them. You may not always react the way you would like, or in a manner you consider ideal, but in the same way that you look at a client's reactions to help define their situation, *the way you react defines you*. The way you react may not be appropriate, but you have to be aware of it and acknowledge it. You will lose your way only when you do not acknowledge your feelings.

When you reach the stage in the interview where you are empathising and getting close to your client, it is crucial that you remain separate, in order to avoid an *identification* with the client. At this stage you are trying to *get into their head while remaining in yours*. If, however, you get too close to the client and 'identify' with them, ie, you want to solve their problem yourself, you are no longer operating objectively from your head, but are seeing things from inside their head only. While you are in their head, you cannot help them, because you are in the same position as they are. In order to help a client effect change, you have to remain 'in *your* head'.

Remaining objective, or 'in your head', is not the same as being distant. It means recognising and respecting your own individuality, as well as that of the person you are helping. It involves a knowledge of the kinds of reaction that may arise, and the kind of sensitive self discipline that is necessary to sort out these feelings, without experiencing guilt over having the feelings in the first place.

When you can distinguish your own feelings, and can tolerate and deal with them without impatience or excessive fantasy, you can also see other people as separate individuals. Here is a checklist of questions to help you recognise some of the signals:

- What is behind my above average interest in this person?
- What am I trying to get from this relationship that I would not like to admit to myself?
- Am I always ready to argue with this person... or always ready to agree?
- Do I overreact to statements that they make?
- Is there a reason why either I or the other person is always late?
- Do I feel bored with them?
- Do I find myself wanting to end the relationship or to hold on to it even though it should end?

These issues are of benefit to the manager, not only in the counselling situation, but in day to day management issues.

The more self aware a manager is, the better their decision making and staff management.

So what do you need to be aware of? One of the most important methods for personal development, is learning how to learn and deal with mistakes. As we have already said, to be an effective counsellor, you have to know and understand yourself. The following ideas summarise things that are written in some textbooks, but you only get to *know* in life itself. They are not laws or commandments, but frameworks for personal understanding and development.

■ Listen to the client

In normal circumstances, the client is not there to outwit or humiliate you. Even when they seem to do nothing but this, they are going through a process which may have little to do with you as an individual (see Chapter 10). They really do want to describe their situation to you. Many of the problems arise because the counsellor cannot, or does not, listen to what the client says.

They frequently tell you what you are missing, in a variety of ways. They may interrupt you and say, 'No, that's not what I mean at all,' or 'That's close to what I mean, but it isn't quite right'.

Sometimes they let you know by not saying anything. This is normal feedback from people who feel their message has not been received. If people feel their words will be misinterpreted, they have no reason to continue their story. Sometimes they try again, sometimes they just close up.

What are some of the signs that people are feeling unheard? Uses of phrases like:

Yes, but... (this means no...)
Well, that might be so, but...
Well, let me put it another way...
No, it's not that...

Here is an example of a member of staff talking to his manager. He is saying that there is something wrong that he would like to correct.

Mr A Well, I don't know what to make of it. I get up in the morning, I want to do my best, have a good day. Then I get down to breakfast, and before I know what is happening, I'm having a quarrel with my wife.

Manager I suppose you're upset because you've been having trouble with your wife.

Mr A No, it's not that. It's more that I don't seem to be able to avoid arguments. I'll be sitting in the coffee lounge and for no reason at all, I react to something someone says and end up arguing over something trivial.

Mr A is trying to communicate his frustration with a seeming lack of self control. While this could be seen as an example of not reflecting the question skilfully, the manager is also seizing on a specific example, and responding directly to the incident, not the global feelings. In this case, the client helps the counsellor by changing the example.

So why did the manager miss the message? This happens to veterans as well as novices. Sometimes the counsellor is listening to something else. Sometimes they have expectations of what the person might say, or what their problem is, and the assumption will take over. (Sometimes the problem may be too close to home for the counsellor...)

One way of checking whether you are hearing the client is if, at the end of the session, they are still trying to say the same thing they were saying at the beginning of the session.

CONCENTRATE ON THE PERSON, NOT THE PROBLEM

There is a great danger of focusing on the problem, rather than the person who is experiencing it. *Problems do not exist in a vacuum.* There are only *people with problems*, and your response should be to the person. If you concentrate too much on the problem, you run the risk of distorting the situation, or even looking at the wrong problem.

You do not have to solve the problem: you only have to help other people accept that responsibility for themselves.

The problem can only be understood in the context of the person who experiences it. If you get the individual into the correct focus, you will automatically get the problem(s) into an accurate perspective.

The less a counsellor feels obliged to 'solve a problem', the more freely they can communicate the strength and support that the client needs, in order to find a solution for themselves. It is a great relief for counsellors to realise that they do not have to solve every problem, or have an answer for every difficulty. Apart from allowing the counsellor to leave responsibility for the situation with the client, it is worth remembering that very few 'problems' have 'solutions'. There is very rarely a formula that a client can pick up, look at and say if I do that, then this will happen. Most of the time, the counsellor's role will be to help a client understand, accept and learn how to deal with their situation.

■ Success is not in your hands

It is common for bright people to want to 'do well'. There is nothing wrong per se with the desire to achieve. What has to be considered is how much that desire can interfere with helping others. What are the elements of this need, or motivation?

Frequently, people who want to do well at all costs view others as opportunities for achievement, rather than as individuals. These people find it hard to look at life without the feeling that they must produce and earn gold stars, or else they will be deemed unworthy. They perceive 'value' as something that only someone else has the power to give them. They do not believe it to be inherent in themselves. Because of this lack of belief in themselves for what they are, they find it necessary to emulate an 'expert'. This makes it very hard for them to be natural, or creative with a client. They are also so aware of the need to prove themselves, that it overrides their ability to see people objectively and as individuals. This need is not a conscious need, but it is important for the counsellor to know it exists.

The personality of the counsellor is their chief asset: you have to know the personality before using it to full effect.

■ Don't rescue

Some people have a need to rearrange people's lives, and provide them with happy endings. This raises several issues:

- Whose needs are being met – the counsellor's or the client's?
- What are you doing for others when you tell them what they should or should not do?
- What are you doing for yourself when you tell others what to do?
- Whose situation or problem is it when you take over?
- The need to take over is not confined to the new counsellor. Old hands frequently feel the need to 'take control'.

You do not help the client by taking over. In doing this, the problem becomes *yours* not theirs. If anything goes wrong with your solution, the blame will be transferred to you. Should everything go well, the client will not perceive it to be *their* achievement, and will not fully understand what has happened. It will therefore be very difficult for them to gain any insight into their own behaviour, or transfer any learning to a new situation. It may make the client more vulnerable or *dependent*. This means that the next time an issue arises they will come back to the counsellor to tell them what to do. They are relying on someone else to tell them what to do. This is not personal growth. The client may have an instant answer to their situation, but no understanding. It is important to question, not only the client's dependence on the counsellor, but also the counsellor's dependence on the client.

- Why do you feel the need to tell the client what to do?
- Does it make you feel stronger in yourself, being able to tell others what to do?
- Do you want to show them (and yourself) how much you know, or how capable you are?
- Do you need to show them (and yourself) how powerful you are?
- Is there an unconscious attraction to the client?

All these thoughts, unpalatable as they may seem, are often around the counsellor's mind. They are perfectly reasonable in the light of the human's need to be approved of and liked. In the counselling situation they have to be controlled so that your needs are of secondary importance to the client's. This increased self awareness is an extremely important by-product of the counselling process for the counsellor. It has obvious implications for the manager in terms of self development. They stand to gain almost as much as the client in those terms, but must always keep their needs in perspective.

The aim of helping others through counselling is that the insights people gain will not only be useful in the specific situation but also in other situations. As a counsellor, it is important that you respect the client's potential to put into perspective what they are feeling, with your *guidance*, not your advice. Each individual has a different level of potential; some only need to verbalise a problem and they can see what they have to do; some take a fair amount of structured guidance. The counsellor has to assess this with each individual, while maintaining each time the basic tenet that it is the client's situation, not the counsellor's.

In management terms, this can sometimes seem difficult. If, for example, someone has a problem relating to work performance, it may not be possible, with time constraints, to allow them the total freedom to 'let them be'. It is important to keep that as an ideal, but bear in mind that is a grey area of 'suggestion' between giving advice and 'letting them be'.

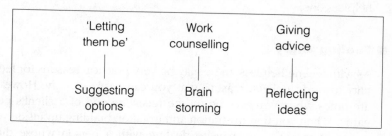

It is crucial for the counsellor to understand why they react in a particular way towards a client. For example, on one occasion, I watched someone trying to switch on a computer printer. They tried the switch twice, each time not quite turning it far enough. The third time they tried, they slammed their fist down on the printer, then turned the switch far enough. The printer sprang into action, and they mumbled, 'The stupid thing only works when I hit it.'

Misunderstanding and/or misreading actions or reactions makes it hard to understand or deal with situations, as you are not working with accurate information. So it becomes easy for the counsellor to end up achieving 'solutions' without solving or even identifying the 'problem'.

So what do other people make us feel, that could damage the communication? When you ask yourself the question, 'What is this person doing to me?', you begin to listen to the feelings that the person arouses in you. This is an important stage in both your development as a counsellor, and progressing your client. It puts the relationship in perspective, and protects you from inaccurate interpretation and inappropriate self interest. You may be wondering how on earth you could get such complex dynamics when you have just called someone into your office to 'talk things through'. They will be there to a greater or lesser degree, depending on the relationship you have with the person, how skilled you are, the type of situation you are dealing with. Let's look at some examples of the reactions you may feel.

■ Feeling helpless

This is a feeling that there is nothing you can do, that you have missed something, or are lacking knowledge or training. These may be perfectly valid explanations for the feeling. There may also be times when you feel helpless, but can't quite work out where it's coming from. One of the most common occurrences of this happens with the person who is passive and dependent, and who acts out a helpless role with everyone. If people do not want to accept responsibility for themselves or their actions, they often, unconsciously, act in a helpless way. This can be infectious, and as a counsellor you are particularly vulnerable to this kind of behaviour, if you are under pressure from other commitments, or are not fully aware of your own emotional reactions. Recognising what is happening is the first step to dealing with it. In this case, understanding why you feel helpless makes you feel *less* helpless, and more in control. It helps to underline exactly who is the helpless one.

■ Feeling angry

As with feeling helpless, there may be very practical reasons for feeling hostility towards a client, reasons that you can easily identify. However, there are times when you may be on the receiving end of a client's personality game. When you find frustration and irritation building up inside you for no apparent reason, you may be dealing with a person whose difficulty is 'passive aggression'.

This problem manifests itself in a style that communicates hostility in a seemingly non-assaultive and indirect way. The problem can be seen in the reactions of others, and of course in yourself, because what you experience is what everyone else is experiencing. The clients with this problem are usually unaware that there is anything wrong with their behaviour, and may not understand why they have difficulties with relationships at work. Passive aggression is one of the most frequently reported reasons for counselling at work, and staff are referred by their bosses, usually because of problems about how they relate to others. They do not experience any anxiety, and so are not very strongly motivated to change their behaviour. (They do not see it as a concern.) They will do things like turn up late for meetings, cancel at the last minute, or agree to something in principle, but not commit themselves. They seem to know how to be unco-operative at the moment when it will do the most harm. They hurt others, not by doing things, but by failing to do things. This thinking goes on at a psychological level of which they are not aware.

This is a very common situation, and it is difficult not to be affected by this style of behaviour. It is important that you are aware that the anger you are experiencing may be coming from the client's 'camouflaged' behaviour. Unless you can understand that your anger is a response to the invisible 'passive aggression' of the client, you run the risk of expressing your hostility in a way that is inappropriate, and may damage the relationship. Once you recognise the behaviour, you will feel more in control of your feelings and see the situation in a clearer perspective.

■ Feeling frightened

This may not happen as often as feeling angry, but is nevertheless something to be aware of. When you cannot find the source of your uneasiness, you may be dealing with a particularly complex personality, which may demand a referral (see Chapter 13). The kind of person we are describing has the power to make people feel uneasy. This comes from the hostility that is buried just underneath the surface of what appears to be an 'intact' self presentation. They may appear distant, but also quite impressive, especially on first association. This quickly wears thin, and as Mackinnon and Michels noted, 'As people know him better, they like him less'. They can change the atmosphere in a group, and can make others argumentative and resentful although they sometimes seem obsessed with fairness and 'being fair'. Although there is no one close to them, they can be acutely sensitive to the feelings of others. They generate a feeling of suspicion that keeps other people on their guard.

There are many reasons for this behaviour, and in this chapter, we are flagging it up as a potential issue for the counsellor to be aware of. This cannot be done unless you listen and understand yourself.

■ Feeling depressed

This is an issue which demands careful thought by the counsellor. It normally happens as a result of frustration or anger with a client, that you cannot express in the interview. Subconsciously, the anger gets turned in on yourself, and you become depressed. Many clients will actually try to irritate or anger you; this is a way of them feeling more powerful than the person to whom they have come for help. Not only does it make them feel superior, but it also allows them to avoid dealing with their own issues. They seem to have an uncanny knack of working out exactly what will wind the counsellor up. Some of the things they say are subtle put-downs, designed to find the counsellor's Achilles' heel.

For example, phrases like:

'I don't suppose you would be able to deal with that...'
'That's not really your speciality, is it...'
'Well, if that's what you think...'
'I don't seem to be able to get my message across...'

Part of you knows that it is not appropriate for you to get hostile with the client, so you repress the feeling, and it frequently emerges as depression or discouragement. The client's objective in this is not clear to them. They are also operating like this at a subconscious level. The client will only realise that this is what they are doing, and its implications, if the counsellor is aware of this process, and can read behaviours accurately. They then need to explain it to the client.

When you cannot find reasons for your reactions, it is very easy to be drawn to feel what the client is trying to make you feel, because it seems to be the only path on offer. This 'joining in' with the client is sometimes called '*collusion*'. Therefore an understanding of the processes is essential not only to avoid tension and stress in the counsellor, but also to enable the counsellor to feel they can deal with the situation itself.

The idea of the client turning all their complicated and unresolved problems on to the counsellor is called *projection*. It is also possible for an inexperienced counsellor who is experiencing some problems of their own, to 'project' their problems on to the client.

It is reassuring for counsellors to understand that their feelings are not 'all their own fault', and that their confusion is not just a product of their inadequacy in the situation. Understanding your reactions allows you to see issues in perspective, and to use your skills productively.

Being able to use your own reactions is a crucial part of the counselling process, and should be seen as a challenge to be mastered, rather than a barrier. Managers and counsellors who learn to listen to staff and clients through their own reactions will feel more confident, competent and able to perform more effectively.

13 · Making a Referral

■ Summary

Referring clients is an important issue for counsellors. This is particularly true for managers for whom counselling is only a part of their role. It is important that counsellors understand why they are referring a client. Once the decision to refer has been agreed and understood, it is part of the counsellor's role to be aware of the resources available, and how to contact them.

When referring a client it is important for counsellors to:

- Understand their reasons for referral.
- Be prepared for the feelings they may experience when they refer.
- Understand the mechanics of referral.
- Be aware of local and national resources.

Referring clients to other professionals is an important issue for counsellors. It is especially important for managers who counsel as part of their responsibilities, and who may frequently come across times when it may not be appropriate for them to act as counsellors. There are many situations in the counselling process where the counsellor may feel that the best thing for the counsellor is to refer them on. The way you as a counsellor raise the issue of referral should allow your clients to explore the reasons for the suggestion. You should also ensure that the client feels it is their decision to decide whether or not to follow up the referral suggestion. (Deciding not to has implications for accepting the consequences of doing so.)

Referral may occur at several stages in the interview:

- *When agreeing the initial contract.* It might happen that early on in the initial session, when you are setting the contract and discussing goals and outcomes, it will becomes apparent on listening to the client's expectations that you are either not going to be able to deal with the issue, or it is not appropriate that you deal with it. At this point the counsellor might make a summary, ending with,

   'Based on what you have been telling me, I'm wondering if you should consider seeing... (then state the nature of the referral agency, for example, a careers guidance counsellor.) If you wish to pursue this, I can probably recommend a suitable person.'

It is also constructive to add your reasons, 'My reasons for suggesting this are...'.

- *At the end of the first session.* When you are referring back to your original contract at the end of the first session, you might summarise and say something along the lines of,

   'We've talked about... and it seems that, on the basis of what you have said, it might be helpful for you to consider seeing... (referral agency),'
   and then explain your reasons.

- *When the relationship has been established.* While the mechanics of actually doing the referring at this stage are similar to the other two stages, this stage is more complex than referring in the relationship, which will be changed by referral.

This links on to exploring the feelings that counsellors have, both when making referrals, and in some cases for not making them.

■ Abandoning the person

Some counsellors feel guilty about handing over their clients to someone else. Referral stirs up many feelings about this, particularly in those counsellors who are very hard on themselves, who feel they cannot make a mistake, even the kind that veteran counsellors make. A good referral is not abandoning the individual, but is a recommendation in the individual's best interest.

■ Getting rid of the person

Referral can easily represent more of a solution for the counsellor than the client: for example they may have become resentful that the client ever knocked on the office door in the first place, and just want to be rid of them. This is not true in most of the cases that are successfully referred.

■ Feeling you have failed

Referring a client may generate in you a feeling that you are not good enough, or you have failed, or are letting down the client in some way.

Unless you deal with your feelings about the client before referral, you may give the impression of rejecting the individual with whom you are working. This does not mean you should be hesitant about the referral, this will only make the client feel the same way. This could leave the relationship of the counsellor and the client unsettled and ambiguous. You should not be afraid of letting the client express positive or negative feelings towards you, and should attempt to explore and clarify them. It is important to handle these feelings and not to take them too personally: they are an essential part of the counselling process. People who have a need for close contact with others will find it difficult to deal with these issues, as they feel it may make people dislike them. It is back to your motivation for counselling, and back to the questions 'Who is the counselling for? What is in the best interest of the client?'

Referral should not be seen as a 'cut-off', but rather as a logical outcome of the process the counsellor and client have gone through. Ideally, it should not be a total surprise to the client; it should be perceived by both counsellor and client as a possibility from the outset. This includes telling the truth to the client about the reasons for referral. However embarrassed or bad you feel, it is not appropriate to disguise the reason for the referral. Fabricated reasons never ring true, and a simple statement from the counsellor about why they are making the referral takes very little time and is an expression of an honest relationship.

■ What might be the reasons for referral?

- The counsellor might feel that the needs of the client are beyond their capabilities at that time.
- The counsellor feels that the client needs help on a long term basis, which they may not have time for, nor may it be appropriate.
- The relationship does not seem to be working, despite repeated efforts.
- There may be a personality mismatch between counsellor and client.
- The line management relationship is in conflict with the counselling relationship.

The fundamental principle of referral is that it is always in the greater interest of the individual. The question you have to ask yourself is 'What is the best thing for the client at this time?' You should be willing to answer questions about the referral and explore the client's feelings about it so that clear boundaries are established even though you may be about to end the relationship.

The process of referral ends with the counsellor moving out of the picture, with the establishment of another professional's responsibility for the client. In terms of the manager's role, it is important that they are seen to support the client in the workplace, although the counselling relationship has terminated.

Counsellors should have a collection of names, addresses, and telephone numbers of referral agencies available to them. It is helpful to build up a network of different people with different skills. Internally, these should include people like the company doctor, and named individuals in Personnel and Training departments. There is a list of the major agencies at the back of the book, but it is helpful to compile a local list for yourself. No list is exhaustive, and it is also helpful to make links with caring professionals in the community, who might be able to advise you of other referral agencies. For example, Alcoholics Anonymous can be very helpful in dealing with some of the problems you come up against. A contact at local agencies can relieve a great deal of personal stress from the counsellor. The counsellor who knows whom to call at the right moment is well equipped for referrals.

There are a baffling array of counselling and psychological services available, and it is sometimes difficult for the manager as counsellor to distinguish between them. There is not really a way of legislating for each problem either, so we cannot say, 'If...happens, you should...', because each individual is different. The organisations mentioned in the Appendix should discuss with you the particular situation, and help you assess whether they can provide the appropriate help.

14·*What the Organisation Can Do*

■ Summary

In most organisations, the major casualty in times of change is communication. Yet sensitive communication is the factor which can make the difference between rapid adaptation with an enthusiastic workforce and general disenchantment.

Good personnel policies and practices help. They are complemented by planned, comprehensive programmes of communication. These should include: well-publicised commitment to staff well-being; objective assessment of employee attitudes; special programmes of communication developed in relation to any major change. Introducing equal opportunity and making relocation easier are two major changes which benefit from such planning. Employees can also be encouraged and helped to take care of their own mental and physical health. A counselling service can complement and reinforce the value of all these measures. It needs careful, systematic introduction.

The great changes in working life outlined in Chapters 1 – 4 all carry potential for personal stress with consequent debilitation of the organisation. Whether or not that potential is realised largely depends on what measures the board is prepared to take to mitigate the adverse effects.

In times of change great vigour is required to push through restructuring, introduce new technology and implement new policies and ideas which the situation demands. The lesson has now been learned, sometimes the hard way, that as much energy needs to be put into care and concern for staff as is put into the mechanics of change if expected benefits are to be realised. Even when no major change is occurring, divisions and units may be experiencing stressful times and individuals undergoing stress in ways and to a degree by no means always known to top management.

Many potential difficulties in achieving dynamic change without damaging people can be offset by good personnel management policies and practices. As an example, careful selection, placement and promotion can do much to avert the strains resulting both from inappropriate appointments and also from vague job descriptions of tasks and responsibilities. Job descriptions which are accurate enough to provide a basis for a person specification will also serve to reduce role ambiguities and the conflicts they can provoke. Skilful induction can do much to ensure that newcomers become as happy and useful as possible in the shortest possible time, as well as reducing wastage. Marks and Spencer reduced wastage of trainees on their graduate training schemes by the simple process of seeking selection interviewers' advice as to the type of store which would best suit each candidate. The initially shy benefited from a time in a small quiet store while the overconfident discovered the size of their task in stores in Central London.

Promotion also demands careful matching. It is no longer a question of rewarding those who have shown most diligence or served the longest. Such a policy today can simply result in turning a highly competent and satisfied computer programmer into an ineffective and unhappy systems analyst or a first class salesman into a poor Sales Manager with consequent distress for everyone in the team. The person with appropriate abilities must be put in the post and alternative ways of recognising and rewarding achievements and high performance found for the programmer and salesman.

But something additional to good personnel practices is required if morale is to be sustained in conjunction with flexibility and rapid adaptation to change. What is needed in addition is a very high level of communication and of sensitivity in everyday management. This chapter reviews some practices which may help an organisation to develop this standard of communication and in particular to introduce an effective counselling service.

■ 1. Issue a mission statement

A company determined to maintain creative levels of change while reducing its adverse impacts might begin by making a commitment to that effect. Commitments to avoid involuntary redundancy now frequently accompany statements about closures and mergers. A commitment to reduce other adverse effects of change as far as possible would go further. It would mean an acceptance that the company sees no value in stress, that the 'two-ulcer man' has no place in its hall of fame and that it sees no merit in executives working overtime and at weekends. It would indicate that in accepting responsibility for introducing change the firm equally accepted responsibility for mitigating any of its effects.

■ 2. Taking the attitudinal temperature

It is dangerous to report bad news to one's superiors. Greek messengers bearing news of a defeat in battle were liable to have their heads cut off. Although company messengers receive less drastic treatment, it is hard for bosses to welcome anyone who has nothing but trouble to report, especially when they themselves are under pressure or when they themselves are the subject of criticism.

One large organisation decided for good reason to relocate several scattered units in one large office building. The pressures of moving on time led top management to skimp on explanations and consultation. Failure to explain why the move was decided upon, how the different groups would benefit and on what terms people would be employed in the new premises led to widespread dissatisfaction. Managers' early warning reports were ignored or subject to the view that, 'everyone would settle down soon.' But long before anyone settled down, absenteeism and sickness rose and 50 per cent of key staff found other jobs. It was a classic case of the message being underplayed by overworked senior management, too preoccupied with the mechanics of change and their own situations to give due attention to the storm signals.

To gather objective information about staff attitudes, companies can commission attitude surveys. An independent consultant can conduct structured interviews with a stratified sample of staff and report on prevailing attitudes regarding a range of issues.

Questionnaires may also be used to yield objective and anonymous evidence of attitudes at different levels. The organisation may choose to design its own questionnaire. With regard to sources of stress, for example, a simple questionnaire might list work elements which are known to be a source of stress (work overload, time pressures and deadlines, travel, poor consultation, attending meetings, office politics, etc.) and ask staff or a random sample of staff to tick the five they find most stressful or to rate each item for stressful impact. A section for any additional sources of stress experienced can provide useful additional information.

Standardised measures of stress are also available. The division of NFER-Nelson concerned with assessment and selection for employment can supply an Occupational Stress Indicator for use in a group or on training courses. The Mast Organisation produced an Organisation Climate Questionnaire by which individual's subjective experience of working in the organisation are translated into general perception of factors such as degree of formal control; amount of initiative permitted; the extent to which good work is recognised; the ease with which communication flows; the quality of contact between individuals; the sense of belonging to a supportive team; the clarity of goals for the organisation and the unit and the expectations regarding work standards.

The organisation can also make use of subordinate surveys. Such surveys might require a subordinate to rate his/her boss in terms of ability to give a clear direction; to supply useful information; to enhance team spirit; to listen and encourage and so forth. A number of ratings by different subordinates are required to ensure anonymity of the individual rater. Scores are amalgamated (by an independent scorer) and the manager given the group result. Subordinate surveys are useful in management training, may indicate areas of potential stress and can help in appraisal. IBM is one organisation which uses peer and subordinate assessments to help pinpoint managers' strengths and weaknesses.

■ Plan for minimal stress

In fulfilment of a mission statement there are a number of steps which every concern can take to maintain morale and commitment whatever changes come to be required:

1. Give plans to reduce impact of change on the staff the same priority as is given to financial plans.
2. Regularly forecast possible sources of stress and plan to mitigate them.
3. Encourage a culture in which individuals accept responsibility for their own mental and physical health and are helped to maintain it.
4. Plan to tackle particular morale problems as they arise, for example;
    i) The introduction of more women into the management team
    ii) The relocation of staff, particularly if going overseas
5. Introduce, promote and support a counselling service available to all staff.

■ When introducing major change

The most important contribution to staff morale is likely to be a thorough and well planned programme of communication, designed to ensure that everyone receives written and spoken explanations of the change, why and when it is occurring and how they will be affected. The programme needs to be timetabled and planned to release accurate information ahead of the grapevine. Especial care must be taken to include those at junior levels in the organisation where the impact of change is least often explained. Managers must have the information to enable them to brief their departments and answer individual queries.

Information clinics, run by senior and respected people, can do much to supplement normal channels of communication or to allay any worries which have developed. When morale dropped in Ford Finance UK, the Chief Executive decided to conduct a canteen clinic once a month. For an hour during the lunch break he visited the canteen, with a promise to answer truthfully whatever questions were put to him. The hostility and fear revealed by the questions at early meetings gradually gave way to greater acceptance and a more constructive approach.

Taking the human factor into account from the outset must also involve retraining plans. A problem encountered by many firms on the introduction of computers has been the long delay between the arrival of the equipment and any realisation of its full potential. Too often it has been assumed that once the new machines are in, all systems will be simplified, all controls perfected and much needed information will instantly be available. In practice, very few benefits are realised until all the staff, from the managers downwards, understand the equipment's possibilities and are to some extent competent in operating it. Retraining staff not only ensures that the equipment is properly used as quickly as possible but also reaffirms the value put upon staff retention.

Since major change gives rise to great feelings of insecurity it is important for the organisation to provide as much security as possible in policies and practices unaffected by change. Hygiene factors such as canteen services and living conditions need to be specially protected. The changes which British industry has seen over the past decade would have been even more traumatic without redundancy pay or redundancy counselling. The flexibility and adaptability of Japanese industry owes much to the strong sense of security provided by a policy of life-long employment. Nissan Motors sets punishing standards of performance; the company's high-fliers are appraised six times a year. But this is within the security of a guarantee of work for the duration of the individual's working life.

■ Introducing equal opportunity

Many organisations are ambivalent in their commitment to equal opportunity. At one level they may appear concerned simply to meet their legal obligations so as to avoid prosecution or adverse publicity, but to have little further interest in promoting real equality. At another, they may make considerable adaptations to existing policy in order to retain the services of highly qualified key women staff.

Neither of these responses do much to prevent the development of strains and difficulties such as the ones described in previous chapters or to foster the good will and commitment which a wholehearted support of equality could achieve.

A full commitment to equality would involve a determined attack upon all procedures which discriminate on any grounds other than relevant ability. It would start with a mission statement asserting the organisation's belief in the benefits of a full realisation of everybody's abilities; its conviction that all doors should be open to ability and its commitment to tackling any evidence of prejudice.

It would involve a determined programme of training and 'on-the-job' experience to ensure that any skills deficiencies due to past discrimination in a group were systematically tackled. It would also involve regular publication of the progress made in developing equal opportunity, for example in increasing proportional representation at every level in the organisation, on training courses and in other opportunities for advancement.

Finally, it would mean a determined onslaught on the secret powers wielded by one-sex traditions and institutions. Marks and Spencer, for instance, helped isolated women managers to counteract male networks by 'legitimising' and assisting in the development of networks of women managers.

■ Making relocation easier

The problems associated with relocation were mentioned in Chapter 3. Simple homesickness is a problem for some. Studies of homesickness have shown that it is not confined to children; it affects people of all ages and both sexes. Ten to 15 per cent of the homesick suffer severely enough to become ill. It does not seem to be especially related to the difficulties of change and occurs even when the new living conditions are an improvement.[1]

Companies which have taken seriously the task of helping staff adapt to overseas relocation have found the following measures helpful:

1. Orientation workshops which the family can attend while still in Britain. Workshops deal with life in the new culture and the possible impact of culture shock. They supply information on host country regulations regarding work opportunities and permits to help a career-minded spouse and give information on health, children's schooling, travel and leisure activities.
2. Written and verbal briefing on the company's own rules and regulations and the support systems they can offer once the family or individual is abroad.
3. Language training to ensure that the traveller arrives with at least a smattering of the language of the host country.
4. Support systems for staff once they are overseas. These may include a local newsletter, perhaps put together by local staff; 'safe mail' facilities similar to the diplomatic bag; introductions to help newly arrived families meet others and join in local life.
5. Provision of some familiar institutions in the new environment. Expatriates clubs were an important feature of life for many serving outposts of the British Empire. International hotel chains deliberately establish identical environments so that, however strange the culture outside, the hotel bar and bedroom shall remain much as they would be at home. Military establishments around the world all have the equivalent of the PX store.
6. Appointing a 'home link', someone with the specific task of helping the overseas family deal with home problems and obtain quick and accurate news of relatives and friends.

■ Supporting positive health

Much can be done to counteract the adverse effects of major change by encouraging individuals to take health seriously and by demonstrating the organisation's commitment to high standards of mental and physical fitness. Medical and personnel staff can be made available to give talks and provide advice on developing a healthy lifestyle. Young people can be encouraged to build into their timetable plans for relaxation, exercise and a healthy diet. The use of outward bound courses can be encouraged. Company sports facilities can bring opportunities for exercise and their use can be encouraged.

A personal health plan may be the first step towards the autonomy that makes possible useful ways of challenging stress at work and of contributing independently and constructively to the well-being of the enterprise.

■ Introducing a counselling service

None of the measures suggested so far need obviate the need for a counselling service. Indeed counselling can be seen as their complement both contributing to their effectiveness and also depending upon them for the realisation of its full benefits. It is through counselling, more than by any other method, that the individual can be helped to an understanding of their circumstances and the organisation can take account of individual need.

The service, like any other new service, needs careful introduction.

1. Early consultation can help to ensure than the service would be welcomed and appropriately used. Early consultation also constitutes the first stage in explaining the service and dispelling any doubts and fears to which it may give rise.

2. A written statement of intent should be issued and well-publicised. It should include statements of support from top management and other influential groups such as the trades unions and the medical department. It should make clear the purpose of counselling and what counselling can and cannot achieve. It should affirm that counselling is not seen as a service only for the ill and mentally disturbed. It should include a guarantee of absolute confidentiality. It should present the counselling service as valuable for both the individual and the organisation.

3. Training programmes and explanatory meetings should be planned for all who may be involved, whether as counsellors or as clients. The aim should be to ensure that everyone has been contacted before they take part in the service.

4. A facilitator of sufficient seniority should be appointed with responsibility for progressing the publicity, the training programmes, the implementation of the service and the monitoring of its effectiveness.

5. The conditions for counselling need to be decided and the decisions promulgated. Questions which need answering include:
   - Will the individual have a choice of counsellor? Must counselling be undertaken only by the individual's superior?
   - If there is to be a free choice of counsellor, what number of clients can a manager/counsellor accept?
   - If external counsellors are to be used, will all counselling be on company premises? Will a counselling room be provided?
   - What are the constraints on counselling? How much time can an individual client spend with a counsellor?
   - How will the benefits of counselling be made known? How will the service be monitored? What measures are planned to ascertain whether the cost of time spent in counselling is being offset by reduced labour turnover, reduced complaints or reduced sickness?

6. On many counts, it may be wise to limit the counselling service initially to a particular group of staff while skills and experience are built up. There must be good reasons for choosing a particular group and there must be expressed commitment to extend the service if it proves useful. Likely candidates for this initial group would be:
   a) New recruits who need help in adjusting to the organisation, the chance to adjust their training programmes or advice in making a choice of department once their general induction training is complete.
   b) High-fliers and potential high-fliers who may benefit from counselling regarding career development plans and the vertical or lateral moves they might make. Included with this group could be experts

brought into the organisation in mid-career and foreigners joining from other countries, all of whom need careful integration.

c) Graduates from company assessment centres, run to encourage self-assessment. Counselling could provide the follow-up service to help an individual come to terms with new self-knowledge.

d) Those facing redundancy or nearing retirement. Counselling may help an individual to adjust to new circumstances. It may also identify abilities available for different types of work or for work in new locations. Older staff may themselves prove valuable as counsellors having more time and possibly more objectivity to give to the task than the full-time line manager can readily command. Older executives may also be much readier to travel and live abroad than are their younger colleagues. Firms who consider overseas work only suitable for the young might recall that the World Health Organisation and the International Labour Organisation recruit most of their overseas consultants from the recently retired.

■ Reference

1. Fisher, S., *Homesickness and Health*, Laurence Erlbaum Associates, 1988.

Appendices

Appendices

Appendix I

Seven Cases for Counselling

■ Case study 1: Terence Thatcher's avoidance of power

After National Service, Terence Thatcher set out to make his fortune. He went into the import/export business with the help of his wife Brenda and a capital of £500. In the 1960s their only child was born, a girl who, unfortunately, suffered from epilepsy. The Thatchers are devoted to her but, apart from her care, they put all their efforts into the company and came to specialise in importing rattan furniture from the Philippines. The business flourished and the Thatchers went frequently to the Philippines during the 1970s looking for new products. Terence relied heavily on Brenda's judgement; she had an excellent eye for attractive new products which would appeal to the retailers they supplied.

By the early 1980s business was highly profitable and it was bought up on very advantageous terms by a national organisation. Terence remained managing director of Thatcher Enterprises and had a place on the main board of the owning company. In 1986 he was within three years of retirement (compulsory at 60) and the board decided that he should relinquish the managing directorship of Thatcher Enterprises in favour of his very able deputy. They asked Terence to take over control of the national credit control department. They considered that his acumen in running his own company and his valuable contribution to board discussions gave a good indication of his ability to handle this department, the chief executive of which had recently retired due to illness.

Terence hesitated before accepting this post, which was not entirely in line with his experience but it was a flattering appointment and an interesting challenge and he eventually accepted. It involved some changes to his life. He had to commute daily to London instead of coming up only for board meetings and he could no longer discuss matters so fully with Brenda. She was, in any event, increasingly preoccupied with the condition of their child, whose epilepsy had worsened.

In the new post

Credit control is a department in which rapid decisions have to be made all the time. Nevertheless, Terence was determined to master the fundamentals of its operations and immediately put a stop on all but the most routine transactions. He spent a great deal of time talking to his subordinates and reading documents. Colleagues began to press him for decisions but for some months put up with his explanation that he was considering radical reforms and needed more time to develop them. Gradually, however, it became clear to an increasing number of his colleagues that he was having great difficulty in agreeing to any decisions at all. He refused to delegate decision making and put off decision making himself by calling for more papers and arranging additional consultative meetings. When colleagues tried to come to see him he was always too busy or not in the office. When subordinates prepared the papers he requested and included recommendations on matters requiring his decisions, he tended to call for more information or sent the paper back with altered terms of reference. At board meetings, when reporting on his reform plans, he would point out a number of small measures he had introduced which reduced departmental costs.

Finally, a colleague decided to confront him. He walked into Terence's office and brushed aside Terence's protests that he was at the moment far too busy to have a discussion. He told Terence that failure to take certain decisions was damaging the business and in particular damaging the colleague's own operations. Terence replied heatedly that he must be allowed time to sort out the real needs of the organisation. When Terence said that he needed further time because of the importance of the decisions requested the colleague said, 'That's not the problem, Terence, and you know it. The problem is that you simply cannot close a deal and you are not making decisions about anything anywhere.' Terence became extremely angry at this and the colleague decided no further useful progress could be made and so left the office and began to think of alternative strategies.

A week later he went round and apologised to Terence and asked if they could drive to a company meeting in the North of England together to sort things out on an amicable basis. Terence agreed and they drove up accordingly. In the course of the journey and a night's stay in a Northern hotel, the colleague put his difficulties to Terence and gained agreement on the measures which he himself required to run his own part of the operation. The colleague remained convinced that Terence was damaging the organisation as a whole by failing to take responsibility for decision making but had concluded that his own best option was to achieve an arrangement which would enable him to continue to operate effectively. Out of loyalty to Terence and recognition of his past contributions to the organisation, he did not take the matter further. In varying degrees similar accommodations were made by Terence's other colleagues and subordinates and people looked forward to the day when he would retire.

Comment

It is easy to see that Terence Thatcher became a victim partly of the board's inadequate analysis of his skills and partly of his own inability to recognise his limitations. He probably also underestimated the effect of the withdrawal of his wife's support and even the removal from his regular working surroundings. He was in a senior position where it was very difficult for him to admit to any inadequacy. What was originally a reasonable request for time to master a new situation appeared to become a complicated defence mechanism against acknowledging his inadequacies.

In this particular situation, Terence had enough credibility through his past achievements in the organisation for his manager to make allowances for him. His age and proximity to retirement may also have been a factor in people deciding more or less to let the matter ride.

Nevertheless, counselling by an external counsellor might have enabled Terence to acknowledge his difficulties in mastering the new job and his limitations. If this could have been achieved he might then have been able to speak more frankly about his difficulties to colleagues whose loyalty and respect for past performance he still commanded.

■ Case study 2: Harry Portree's need to be loved

Harry Portree is the personnel director of a well known confectionary firm. After obtaining a first in classics he remained with his old university for some years as a lecturer.

He established a reputation as an entertaining and able lecturer and was extremely popular with the undergraduates. He was also very popular with university colleagues and had a wide circle of friends. After some time he felt stifled by the routine of teaching. He looked at pursuing a higher degree, but decided he did not feel motivated enough. This decision ensured that he could not progress in the academic field. He was also feeling that he had mastered the challenge of teaching undergraduates and should now look for new vistas. His skills with people and ability as a teacher had been amply confirmed and he was able to move from university life to the position as training manager and supervisor of the inductions programme for graduates in the confectionary firm where he is still employed.

His work as training manager was characterised by inventiveness and great presentational skills and, once again, he was extremely popular particularly with his more able colleagues and with the graduate intake. He was less effective in maintaining paperwork and following up on projects and programmes for which he was responsible. However, his boss greatly valued his outstanding abilities which were particularly important in a company whose managers were predominantly young, intellectually able and highly qualified. Eventually Harry progressed to the stage where he was given his own secretary. She was a competent older person who admired him. Thereafter his weaknesses were largely taken care of and his special skills could be deployed in wider fields. He was made a training director for the whole organisation and in his mid-forties was promoted to personnel director.

While at university Harry had married a member of the administrative staff a few years older than himself. Angela was a forceful woman strongly committed to moral rearmament. In due course they had four children. Angela ran their home efficiently and found time to travel up and down the country preaching to moral rearmament and non-conformist groups. She also made television appearences and broadcasts so that she developed something of a national reputation.

Harry is gently and charmingly deprecating about his wife's activities whenever they are mentioned by his working colleagues. But she organises their home efficiently and takes most of the responsibility for looking after the children.

Harry's contribution to his company remains consistent. He is a quick-witted, inventive and charming member of the Board and his lack of interest in routine and paperwork is to a large extent made good by his efficient secretary and competent subordinates.

The current situation

There are, however, drawbacks to this situation. He irritates some colleagues. They are tired of the number of occasions when Harry has failed to bring the correct papers to a meeting because he has picked up the wrong bundle from his desk or alternatively has not returned to his office in time to collect them.

His subordinates are uneasy at the number of occasions when he has failed to deal with difficult issues. As an example, it recently became necessary to dismiss a senior member of staff. Harry had a discussion with this person which he said constituted a verbal warning. He subsequently wrote the individual a letter which he claimed amounted to a written warning. When these measures failed and the time came to see the individual and dismiss him, Harry was on a protracted tour in Europe and left the task to his deputy, Eleanor Partridge.

Eleanor saw the individual concerned and explained why she was taking Harry's place. The employee protested that he had not understood that his interview amounted to a verbal warning and the letter was certainly not a written warning. He showed the letter from Harry and there was no doubt that there remained considerable ambiguity over its interpretation. Eleanor had faced similar situations before and was far from happy. On this occasion, she asked to see the Managing Director in strict confidence and expressed some of her unease.

As another instance, the work of the training department is supposedly heavily modified by the information coming back from the appraisal interviews which are conducted annually with all staff. Some departments are sadly behind with supplying this information and the training manager asked Harry to lend weight to his requests for an improvement in returns. Harry promised to do this but failed to do so for some weeks. The training manager then wrote a tough letter to go to the renegade departments which he asked Harry to sign. Harry put the letter in his in-tray and said he would consider the matter, but was not sure that this was quite the right tone to take. The letter has now been in his in-tray for ten days.

As a final example, the board proposed some months ago to introduce a payment by result scheme for production staff. This move will not be popular with the trade union officials, but the production manager says many staff would welcome it. Harry has always got on well with the trade unions officials, as he does with everyone. However, he agreed to review a number of schemes and to put up proposals appropriate for the firm. The production manager is extremely anxious to introduce this scheme and start staff discussion about it. He has spoken to Harry and Harry claims that he has now gathered a great deal of information on the subject and has a paper in draft, but is most anxious to get just the right tone and not ruffle too many feathers. Finally, the production manager went to the managing director and complained that if he could get hold of the material, he could work out a scheme himself but Harry will do nothing himself and won't hand it over. The managing director took the matter up with Harry. With his usual charm, Harry replied that his paper was indeed nearly ready and would be submitted to the next board meeting.

Comment

The persistent theme in Harry's life history is one of capitalising on his strengths and making no attempt to tackle his weaknesses. His strengths are so considerable that he does achieve many successes and gains the co-operation of people prepared to make good his deficiencies. However, he is now in a position where his failure to confront difficult issues and face up to unpopularity can no longer be overlooked.

Could counselling help? Harry is highly intelligent and in many respects a sensitive person. He might be helped by an external counsellor to recognise his own fear of the hostility which confrontation might bring. From this he might come to consider a move to some position in the organisation where his talents could be used and his defects would not be so damaging.

Changing his behaviour and becoming able to confront others, however, is a bigger issue. A counsellor might conclude that referral for psychotherapy would be the correct course of action and Harry would have to agree to this.

■ Case study 3: Philip Bailey's need for security

Philip Bailey runs the central administration department for Helpers Limited, a group of private rehabilitation and respite clinics. He joined the firm 12 years ago at the request of its founder, Jim Metcalfe. At that time, the enterprise consisted of one 15 bed nursing home offering general nursing care. Within a few years the nursing home became a rehabilitation centre for patients recovering from orthopaedic and heart surgery and strokes. Four other homes were opened, one offering rehabilitation services and three offering respite care. The respite centres take in, either overnight or for short stays, elderly and mentally and physically handicapped people living at home. Their prime function is to provide relief for the patients' relatives.

Charges to patients are not excessive and all the homes are well run by good staff. The rehabilitation homes are respected and recommended by surgeons and there is a waiting list of potential clients for the respite centres.

Helpers Ltd has done well enough to provide from profits most of the capital for starting up new units.

Jim Metcalfe remains the prime mover in the business. His outlook is philanthropic and he has never been greedy for personal financial profit. He has come to rely heavily on Philip and is always generous in his acknowledgment of this. They have more or less divided the running of the business between them. Jim takes on the external contacts which involves: negotiations for new properties; their restoration or reconstruction as necessary; dealing with local authorities, health authorities and the requirements of doctors or paramedicals; and appointing the director (matron) for each home. Philip has taken on responsibility for running the central office; keeping the accounts and dealing with the external accountants and bank managers on a day to day basis; staffing the central office and assisting the directors and matrons in appointing the rest of the staff in the homes. He has approved budgets for the homes in consultation with Jim. Although he does not deal with the external authorities, his responsibilities have involved him in fairly regular visits to all the homes and he is well known to the staff everywhere and to many of the patients.

Philip Bailey considers that Helpers Ltd offers an important service and is very proud of the contribution he has made to its growth and success. In this respect his visits to the homes are very important to him. They reassure him that Helpers Ltd is undertaking valuable, badly needed work. In addition, he feels enormous sympathy for the patients and for their relatives who he meets from time to time. His empathy for their situation is heightened because of his own circumstances. Philip was the only child of an unmarried mother and was brought up in poor circumstances. He was a small, rather frail child and his present height, 5′ 2″ is well below normal. He suffered a good deal at school from bullying on account of his stature and became quite solitary and dependent on his mother's company. On leaving school he took a job with the local bank. Going into the bank was respectable and safe and his mother was very proud of him for obtaining the position. However, he was not happy. As an intelligent and diligent young man he did well but he continued to feel that banking was not the life for him and to find the attitude of customers and the other staff alien. They were dominated by money and not sufficiently caring. He was therefore extremely thankful when Jim Metcalfe, one of the bank's customers, suggested he might join Helpers Ltd.

Philip had been with Helpers Ltd for three years when he suffered two painful experiences. He had been courting a local girl and eventually plucked up courage to ask her to marry him. The girl turned him down and when he persisted told him that the real impediment was his physique. He has not formed any relationships with women since then. Later that year his mother fell ill; her cancer was diagnosed late and she died within four months. Philip saw no reason to leave the flat which he had shared with her and he continues to live there alone. His social life outside work is very limited.

Jim Metcalfe was extremely sympathetic and supportive at the time of Philip's mother's illness and Philip has become highly dependent on this relationship and on the satisfactions which his job brings him.

Recent developments

Jim has American cousins whom he visits fairly regularly. A year ago he introduced into Helpers Ltd his 23 year old nephew Edmond. Edmond had not found any work he enjoyed in the States and came over by family agreement to study his uncle's business and see if managing this type of enterprise suited him. Edmond is a short, jolly, fat, cheerful young man with an interest in everyone and an excellent sense of humour. He rapidly became very popular with staff, both at head office and in all the homes. Jim also became very fond of him and they saw a good deal of each other socially outside business. Jim arranged for Edmond to visit the homes regularly in order to gain experience and also increasingly invited him to come on visits to the external authorities.

At first Philip helped Edmond in every way he could. He liked the young man and wished to help Jim. He also assumed that Edmond would shortly return to America. However, this situation has been changing. Edmond appears to be settling in. He has acquired an English girlfriend who has turned up at the office from time to time to drive him off in her sports car. Recently he was invited to a private party given by one of the matrons. Philip was not; he heard about the event inadvertently through a chance remark in an office conversation and was extremely hurt. On another occasion, Philip met a deputy matron coming into the head office and learned from her that she had come to see Edmond. It appeared that Edmond had told her and others that they could always come to see him, as he was trying to reduce the load which Philip carried. When Philip confronted Edmond about this, the latter replied that he had indeed said this to several people but had thought he was only being helpful. Philip found himself doubting if this was true.

As a further instance of what Philip was beginning to see as an encroachment, Jim recently informed Philip that he and Edmond had been to see a new property and were completing negotiations for its purchase and the papers would be coming through shortly. Jim explained that he had taken Edmond along because he had said he was at a loose end while Philip was clearly busy.

This was the first occasion on which Jim had excluded Philip from early discussions and negotiations and Philip had reacted angrily. Jim had expressed himself as very surprised at Philip's annoyance. He had reminded Philip how much he relied on him and pointed out to him the tremendous authority and responsibility he carried in Helpers Ltd. Philip had then asked for a definition of his responsibilities in relation to Edmond and Jim had agreed that this was a matter which would have to be sorted out. Meanwhile, said Jim, Edmond was still learning the business and the situation was 'fluid'.

Over the last few months Philip has become angrier and angrier. He talks less to staff than he used to do and makes fewer visits to the homes. When he does talk to people he tends to be abrupt and to confine his remarks to work practicalities. Some of the junior staff are becoming fearful of going to ask his advice. One or two more senior people have mentioned this to Jim, who notices what is going on but feels uncertain about how to tackle it.

Comment

Philip's situation is typical of someone who has worked competently for a long time in rather a narrow situation using a particular management style. Such a person can easily be outflanked by someone with additional talents and wider experience. The situation is clearly too awkward for Jim to deal with, since he has divided loyalties. Nevertheless, he owes Philip a good deal and could accept some responsibility for helping him. Philip does need help if he is to recognise both his real strengths and his real limitations. He also needs to understand how his present reactions are exacerbating his problems. Counselling could help this process and free him to make decisions about his situation. He might be helped to adopt a less dependent management style and to develop and use the skills of assertion and confronting, so that he can deal with Edmond. He might then be able to clarify his position and make it more secure.

■ Case study 4: Laetitia Branksome keeps up appearances

Laetitia is a handsome person in her mid-forties. She works as a buyer in a well known department store. She has made fair progress in view of the fact that she joined the store only ten years ago, one of the recruits resulting from a drive to attract people seeking a change of occupation.

Laetitia's first career was as a school teacher. Both her parents were dedicated teachers and as a young person she never seriously thought of any other career for herself. After training, she took a number of posts including one or two overseas. Eventually she settled down at a girl's public school where she finally became head of the mathematics department. Although reasonably happy, she had come to realise that further advancement was unlikely and had grown increasingly dissatisfied with the poor level of teacher's pay. She had also encountered problems arising from her liaison with the Art Master, a charming young man who lived in a caravan with his wife and small daughter on the edge of town. Her relationship with him became known and school and town sympathy was on the side of the Art Master's family. Her parents were sorry when she decided to leave teaching and somewhat shocked when they heard about the Art Master.

When she applied to join the store, Laetitia impressed the recruiters with her good qualifications and smart appearance and these continue to be valuable assets. She is always exceptionally well groomed and turned out and always maintains a friendly, cheerful, competent manner. She has a large flat in Wimbledon which she shares most of the time with Bob Hanston, a librarian whom she met on the train commuting into work. What Bob admires most about her, he says, is her effortless competence. She does everything so well, he says, and runs the flat and her job so beautifully – in contrast to his estranged wife who lives with their two children in a small house in Putney. He visits his wife from time to time and always returns very irritated by the state of the house and the children's lack of manners. Laetitia does not conceal her relationship with Bob and sometimes laughingly says she wonders what would happen to it if she was not so careful to keep up her appearance and her house-keeping standards.

Laetitia also prides herself on contributing to the store in ways which are additional to carrying out her job. She was elected to the sports and social committee some years ago and has served on it ever since. She is on a panel of speakers for visiting local schools and telling school leavers about job opportunities in the store. These activities ensure that she is always busy and that she is well-known to many people.

The present situation

Despite these contributions, Laetitia is not popular. Some are put off by so much apparent competence. Others wonder how real the competence is. Members of the sports and social committee have noticed that, although Laetitia always turns up to meetings and talks a lot, she has not taken office, does not undertake any of the administration required between meetings and has not proved a reliable support in helping to organise events. She also refers rather often to her many years of membership.

As a buyer, Laetitia has placed orders late and has made some mistakes in selection. Her supervisor, the section manager, has discussed these issues with her; he is a man who relies on reasoned discussion and explanations in improving staff performance and he has explained the store's requirements carefully. Somehow this method does not seem to work with Laetitia. She responds with enthusiasm and then explains volubly why any mistakes have occurred. They are never her fault.

Recently, after another poor selection, the superior changed tactics and simply ordered her to consult him when selecting new merchandise. She resented this very much. However, she has consulted him from time to time since, explaining to everyone that it's just because he is very pernickety and she has to go along to humour him. Her colleagues are skeptical; they note that she appears not to accept how serious a criticism it is for a buyer to be monitored in this way.

Comment

Laetitia seems driven by a powerful need to appear faultless. In everything she devotes much time and energy to appearances. In contrast she seems much more casual about the substance of what has to be done.

Her history suggest some possible explanations. For instance, she has left her first profession, disappointing her parents in the process. She may need to reassure herself that she made the right career decision in coming into store work. She has experienced one unhappy relationship with a married man and may feel much is at stake in this second relationship; it has, of course, some parallels.

Laetitia would probably find it difficult to accept that she needs the sort of assistance counselling could provide. Nevertheless, a supportive, constructive counselling session could help her. It might enable her to recognise the anxieties which require her to appear perfect. Once she has acknowledged her fears, she might be able to understand them and then either to discard them or to contain them in some way less damaging to herself. Her supervisor seems the only person who might be able to counsel her without arousing the alarms which suggestions of external counselling could bring.

■ Case study 5: Clara Westby suffers a bereavement

Clara Westby is one of two partners running a small, successful estate agency. She and her partner, John Carew, went into business five years ago and did very well out of residential properties in Essex and East Anglia. Business has not been so good lately and they are thinking of joining forces with a small company in France where sales of country properties remain buoyant.

This is John's idea. He has always been the partner with the new ideas and the capacity to spot an opportunity. He needs to work with someone who is a sound administrator with a good head for figures and it was because she possesses these abilities that he asked Clara to join him when he was setting up his own business. He knew her work well; they had been together for some years in the Exeter office of a nationwide estate agency and had kept in touch when Clara moved to the firm's Saffron Walden office. Indeed, it was while visiting Clara and her new husband that John's ideas for setting up on his own with her help finally crystallised. He and the man with whom he lives had been charmed by the countryside around Clara's cottage and had found themselves a beautiful country house in Suffolk.

He persuaded Clara that together they could set up a successful business which would give her more autonomy and a very much larger income than she could hope to achieve working for her present firm. The appeal for Clara was that her new husband was proving an unreliable breadwinner given to bouts of alcoholism. Although a naturally cautious person she had eventually been convinced by John's arguments and joined him in the hope of securing a good financial basis for her family.

Clara Westby was born Clara Jones in a small village outside Cardiff. She attended the local girls' school and left with one 'A' level to go straight to secretarial college. As soon as she had completed her secretarial course she joined the local office of the estate agency which employed her until she left to join John. She soon proved herself a sensible, capable person and was offered a promotion if she would transfer to the Exeter office. She regretted leaving her parental home, but decided to move on finding that an old school friend living in Exeter could offer her a bedsitting room in her flat.

This arrangement worked well for about 18 months and Clara then met a local businessman some ten years older than herself. She moved into his flat and they made plans to marry. After a few months, Clara became pregnant and they agreed to move the date of the marriage forward. Clara returned to Cardiff to make all the arrangements with her family and phoned home every night to report progress. She had expected to be away for a fortnight but after ten days she was unable to get an answer from the flat. She returned to Exeter early to find the flat empty with a note from her boyfriend explaining that he had used an assumed name while living with her and that he was already married and was now leaving the district.

In the next few months Clara discovered that the flat rent was in serious arrears and that he had not paid gas, electricity and telephone bills although she had handed over her half share. She discussed the matter with her employers who agreed to help her with an advance and she also received money from her parents. One way and another she managed to pay off the debts and to prepare the flat for the new baby. In due course her daughter was born, Clara's younger sister came to live with her to look after the child and Clara went back to work.

All these experiences taught Clara a great deal. She became a meticulous administrator who managed her home and her job by careful adherence to routine. She became scrupulous over money and very concerned to ensure a secure income for herself and her child and to keep tight control over all family expenditure. The office benefited greatly from her concerns and, indeed, she was much admired for the way in which she had coped with her difficulties. It was at this time that her present partner began to think of her as a possible future colleague.

Matters did not work out so well on the home front as Clara's younger sister soon rebelled against the precise regime she was supposed to follow. They agreed to part and Clara accepted an invitation from the company to move to the Saffron Walden office where she understood she could find domestic help and there was more chance of a place for her daughter in an infant school. She rented a small cottage in a village outside the town and found a local babysitter who looked after the little girl well. The cottage had a half acre garden and Clara developed an interest in growing vegetables. This led to frequent visits to the local garden centre which was run by Tim Westby.

Tim was single, younger than Clara and possessed of an easy-going charm. He began to visit the cottage and became very fond of the little girl and reliant upon Clara's good sense and good advice on running his business. In due course they married and the family was augmented by twin boys.

For a period everything went very smoothly. Tim's business continued to make modest profits while Clara rose to second in command of what was now quite a large office. But the birth of the twins reactivated Clara's concerns over money and organisation and she became more demanding than before, particularly as regards the way Tim ran his business. He reacted with bouts of drinking and by neglecting the business altogether for short periods. It was in this phase of her life that John had turned up and had put the proposal that they go into business together.

The present situation

Setting up the new business involved both John and Clara in working for very long hours. Tim was left on his own with the children and was expected to stand in when the babysitter was not available. One evening when the children had gone to bed and Clara was still not home he began drinking heavily. With still no sign of Clara at half-past ten at night, he decided to go to her office for a showdown. He got into his car and drove furiously down the road. He took a bend too sharply and crashed into an oncoming lorry.

Tim did not die but he was permanently severely damaged both physically and mentally. Within a few months it was clear that he would have to spend the rest of his life in an institution.

It was understandable that Clara should be shattered by these experiences but a year after the accident, her partner John is becoming concerned at the way she is adjusting to them. In particular, she has developed an obsessional attitude towards Tim whom she visits three or four times a week and increasingly describes as the most remarkable man she ever met, a person whose extraordinary talents and brilliance were never properly acknowledged by others. His care must now be given priority over the business and indeed her family. Quite apart from the effects on the office and the children John is concerned for Clara. He wonders what can be done to help her.

Comment

Hitherto Clara has relied on her skills in administration and organisation to cope with her circumstances. When her picture of a conventional, supportive family life was shattered by the departure of her first boyfriend, she reacted by imposing a rigid structure upon a traumatic new situation. When her twin sons were born she dealt with complexities of the new family structure by increasing her control over her husband and children. This solution damaged her relationships, on the first occasion with her younger sister, and secondly with her husband. It could be said to have led indirectly to the present tragedy. She seems to be dealing with her sense of guilt and failure by a deification of the person she helped to damage.

Clara needs help to be brought back to reality and a clearer perception of her own strengths and weaknesses. John's concern for her and his long association with her makes him the best person to initiate this process. She may need more professional counselling than he can provide but his initial counselling could help her to understand something of what is happening and why she needs positive help.

■ Case study 6: Angela Toogood fights dirty

When Angela Toogood joined Classics Limited, she caused something of a stir. She was aged 23 and had obtained an excellent degree from a well-known art college which she had entered late after a brief career as a model. She was small, extremely pretty, outgoing, friendly and amusing.

Classics Limited designs, prints and publishes packaging materials. Originally the firm specialised in sleeves for records. It has now branched out to make packaging for cosmetics, dried foods, herbs and teas. Angela works in the design department which is, in a sense, the heart of the business. Classics Limited is distinguished by the quality and originality of its designs and the designers are an interesting mixture of people – from the racy, trendy group to which Angela belongs to the one or two who are so reserved and wrapped up in their work that they are left alone by practically everybody.

For a while it appeared that Angela could do no wrong. She dropped her old boyfriend and appeared to manage for a while without any particular escort. However, she was seen from time to time going out with a senior man in the legal department and she let drop one or two remarks about the nightclubs they had visited and the distinguished people they had met. Her work was good and on occasion extremely good and when she was taken to meet clients they found her amusing and charming.

A less attractive side to Angela's character first appeared in her treatment of juniors. She was critical and impatient in her dealings with secretaries and on occasion openly contemptuous of the work of young newcomers to the department. At departmental meetings she had a tendency to play down colleagues' ideas and applaud anything approved of by senior people. It has also been noticed that, when working on joint projects, Angela manages to convey that all the original ideas are hers. Understandably some colleagues have become reluctant to work with her.

She tends to work sporadically and on various occasions would still be working when everyone else had left the office. One or two colleagues have begun to wonder about this diligence, especially after one of them returned from holiday to find that Angela had presented a design for a new client which was remarkably like the one he had been working on himself and which he had left in his folder.

At a trade conference it was noticeable that Angela was seen talking exclusively to the most senior people present and ensuring that she was photographed with them for the trade magazines. A woman colleague once commented that she could not understand how Angela could go on flattering the old men about the place and Angela had giggled and said, 'Why not? It's all you have to do. It's so easy, you can get them to do anything you like.' This attitude offended several people. The feminists found it degrading. The other designers, who all value the department's reputation, are beginning to wonder if this matters as much to Angela as getting on by any means and at whatever cost. They do not doubt her ability and do not object to personal ambition but they greatly resent having the department's joint efforts and their own high quality work undervalued by a cynical newcomer.

Angela talks a lot about her glamorous past as a model and the trips to Italy and America which it entailed. She says very little about her family background. However, a junior member of the department who joined Angela's Art School for Angela's last year remembers a student evening when Angela did refer to her early family life. She was the youngest by ten years of six children and was fondly called by her father, 'Little Miss Mistake.' Angela boasted that her brothers and sisters were very jealous of her father's attention. He used to shout for her whenever he came home, which might well be nearly midnight, and she would be got out of bed to go downstairs and greet him. He always brought her a present and she had to open it at once; he expected her to be pleased whatever it was. Angela referred to her father as enormously successful (he ran a chain of delicatessen shops) and her mother as really only interested in babies.

Somebody asked how her brothers and sisters had felt about her father's favouritism and she had giggled again and said they thought she was very spoiled, but anyway she had done much better than them so her father was right. All her sisters had done was get married; they now lived somewhere in the North well away from her parent's home. One brother had gone into the delicatessen business and the other two brothers had gone abroad. She had seen her oldest sister once or twice since joining Classics Limited ('She was the only one I got on with. She was OK') but none of the others.

On one occasion Angela arrived in the office with a suitcase and told everyone that this time she simply had to go to see her parents. Her mother who was bedridden had suffered a slight stroke. She expected it to be a difficult visit because they were always asking her down and she was always putting them off. It transpired that Angela had left home for good when she began her travels as a model. She had taken a flat in London whilst following her art course and had hardly gone home since. 'They make much too much fuss of me, it's really bad for me. Of course, I write and phone and everything but I'm really too busy to get down much. No, I don't invite them up – they'd hate it. Oh well, this time I'll just have to face them.'

The present situation

Angela is posing her head of department with an increasingly difficult problem. She is undoubtedly talented and despite the rumours of plagiarism much of her work is highly original. She remains popular with customers and indeed has established something of a reputation outside the firm as one of the most outstanding designers around.

Within the organisation, her relationships are deteriorating. Although not much is said about it, the rumour is that she no longer sees her lawyer escort and that he broke it off. Colleagues are growing more irritated. One woman recently commented that if Angela spent less time blowing her own trumpet the department would be an easier place to work in. Two people have now explicitly declined to work with her on assignments and she is heartily disliked by all the juniors.

The head of department has talked to her about this and she has replied that she cannot be expected to train juniors while doing work at her level but is perfectly happy to work with real professionals. He has also mentioned that she should consider contributing more to the department and spending less time being seen with senior people. On that occasion she laughed and said, 'Oh, who's been snooping now?' He is seriously beginning to wonder about the balance between her undoubted ability and her disruptive effect on others.

Comment

It is rather easy to see Angela as the sad victim of her early successes and of a childhood which combined privilege with some neglect and hostility. Her 'attractiveness' and charm have probably helped her get away with many behaviours about which colleagues would otherwise have confronted her. The easiest decision for Classics Limited may be to part with her and allow some other organisation to benefit from her talents and continue the process of either helping her to adjust to adult life or confirming her in her present pattern. Alternatively, her boss might try to counsel her and establish with her a relationship in which she can be more honest and realistic about her situation. The risks involved in establishing such a relationship in the workplace with someone like Angela are obvious but as she is still young and clearly very anxious for approval he might be able to persuade her to go on to an external counsellor.

■ Case study 7: Claud Carrick relies on charm

Claud Carrick, aged 47, is the International Sales Director of a medium sized chemical firm, a post he has held for five years. He is a tall, handsome man with a fluency for languages and an easy rather dominant manner. He is married to a school teacher, who has recently been made headmistress of a small public school in the Home Counties. Their two children have virtually left home, one of them to go to university and another to take a course in hotel and catering management. Claud travels a great deal and has a flat in London; nowadays he returns to the family home quite rarely.

In his job, Claud is a tough negotiator who brings in sharply priced contracts, but is equally careful to see that the firm meets its obligations to customers. As a result, overseas customers respect him and despite increasing competition he has retained the custom of many of them over many years. He runs the office back home quite strictly. He is very demanding over working deadlines and standards of presentation and assumes everyone will stay on at work until a job is finished. To be fair, he does the same himself.

But Claud does have a weakness which is his attitude towards women staff. He says that he prefers to work with women and he appoints women to his department in preference to men. When asked how he chooses his staff he replies that they have to have 'big ones' and nice long legs. 'I really can't stand having ugly women around.' Others have noted that they tend to be clever, compliant women of whom he can ask a great deal without paying vast rewards. Most of his staff work very long hours and their rewards are largely in the form of flattery. He also buys a great deal of scent in duty free shops and hands it out in gifts as rewards for exceptional work. He also takes his senior staff out to lunch one by one where he speaks very flatteringly about their contribution and indicates that he finds them highly attractive.

After these lunches, Claud has been known to push through a decision on the grounds that he obtained the individual's agreement in a private conversation. This has happened on a sufficient number of occasions for the staff no longer to welcome his invitations.

When a woman was appointed to the company board he attempted similar tactics; he invited her to lunch, flattered her and then casually assumed they were agreed on controversial issues. She sharply told him off and the atmosphere for the rest of lunch was cool. He has retaliated since with amusingly derogatory remarks about women tycoons and how we poor men can never keep up with them. She cheerfully tells him he is an unregenerate male chauvinist pig.

Otherwise Claud is respected by his fellow directors for his contribution to the organisation and his knowledge of overseas markets. Nevertheless, one or two of them are uneasy about his relationship to his staff. They have heard from a few of the more outspoken women that they resent what they see as Claud's exploitation. The company secretary hears most of this, partly because he is always in his office and partly because he is well liked and discreet.

Claud does not talk about women to his colleagues but he does to junior male staff when they are on sales trips abroad. He then reveals a rather cynical condescending attitude and refers to his 'conquests'. His story of the stir he caused when staying at a nudist camp is by now well known in junior management. Some of his juniors react to these stories by feeling flattered that so senior a person should take them into his confidence. Some are embarrassed and some find his attitude unattractive.

His secretary, looking through his desk diary one morning, was somewhat embarrassed to find tucked in the back a number of postcard sized photographs of women's buttocks. She put them back and said nothing but some time later did mention the find to a close friend in the office and the story has now got around.

The present situation

Recently, a member of Claud's staff asked to speak to the company secretary. She has spoken to him before and he arranged the appointment with some foreboding of what she would say. What she had to say was that there was a good deal of dissatisfaction in Claud's department. The three senior women members of staff had been to see Claud about his behaviour but had been treated to a lot of banter culminating in annoyance that they, 'couldn't take a joke' and 'weren't women in the proper sense.' She told the company secretary that she would have asked to see the managing director if he were ever around, but he never is. Indeed the secretary knows he is very frequently abroad or occupied with meetings involving outside people; even the directors find him hard to track down.

The member of Claud's staff says she has now decided that somebody on the board must understand what is happening in Claud's department. She describes Claud's management style as a mixture of sexual exploitation and sexual harassment serious enough for her and some others to be looking into how to bring a case of sexual harassment against him. She tells the company secretary that she is well aware the board will not want to face up to this problem because of Claud's contribution to the firm. But she would like them to realise how serious it is.

Comment

Claud does indeed rely heavily on sexual exploitation, verging on sexual harassment, as a means of managing his women staff. Although his colleagues have some understanding of what he is doing, his behaviour has little apparent effect on his work and would scarcely be noticeable to them if the staff did not complain. So far, the complaints have been muted and could be dismissed by those unwilling to listen as small irritations.

In her interview with the company secretary, however, Claud's subordinate has raised the matter to a much more serious level and has given the secretary a good reason to pursue it. Indeed he is the only one who can. He could refer everything to the managing director but this would only shelve the problem due to the latter's unavailability and his having no direct evidence to go on. The secretary has, of course, no authority over Claud; he has no great liking for him and they do not meet outside working hours. But he respects Claud's work and they have always co-operated effectively on work matters.

There is therefore some basis for a discussion. Confrontation is unlikely to prove helpful but he might make headway if he invited Claud along to discuss an office problem and then presented the situation neutrally as something they needed to discuss. While Claud's attitude to women is likely to take a long time to change, his attitude to work is responsible and professional. If he can come to see that his behaviour is damaging the work of his department he may be prepared to act differently.

Appendix II

Two Counselling Interviews

1. Cheryl's problem is not what it seems

Interview between Cheryl, a supervisor, and her boss Harry

This interview is in two parts. In the first part Harry discovers that Cheryl's problem cannot be dealt with in ten minutes. They agree to meet for an hour the following day.

Harry Okay Cheryl.

Cheryl Hi Harry.

Harry Hi. Thanks for coming along. I mean, this morning, when we met in the corridor, you said that you would like to grab ten minutes of my time so, here we are. We have ten minutes. Perhaps you'd like to tell me what it is I can do for you.

Harry sets the agenda with a tight time limit.

Cheryl Yes, look I know you're really busy and I don't like to load these sort of things on you really, but I just felt that after I saw you, when I, just before I saw you in the corridor, I'd just had a huge row with my team at a team meeting, and I felt I'd just got to talk to you about it because I, it's just going, it's just, it's just gone too far and it's really the type of people that we're employing, that are not really able and capable of doing the job. I am constantly having to chase them up over work that they're doing, I am constantly having to be behind them saying, 'how are you, what are you doing, come on get on with it'. I've never had to work like this at all Harry. Never! And you know that I've got a good track record. I've worked for the firm a long time. I've never had this problem and it's something about the sort of calibre of staff that have recently been employed that are just not up to the job and I really don't know what to do.

This rambling statement indicates a good deal of anxiety.

Harry That sounds like quite a serious problem. You feel that the team aren't performing as well as they should be?

Harry restates it in terms of Cheryl's feelings.

Cheryl Yes.

Harry And you're, you feel that you're having to push them all the time to do things that they should be doing?

Cheryl Yes, I'm sort of spoon feeding them. I can't, I can't delegate any task completely because they just haven't got the ability to take the responsibility.

Harry It sounds to me like that's maybe the first thing that we need to establish actually is what it is that's making the team perform like that. I mean, you've made one suggestion that perhaps that the people are the wrong people or that they are the wrong calibre as you said. There may be other issues perhaps we have to discuss. You know, things like the kind of work that they're doing, or deadlines, or maybe how you feel.

Harry decides he must get all the facts.

Cheryl Well it's not changed. This work's exactly the same; you know we've been working for this company for 13 years now Harry, and it's not like I'm a new girl. I know the job, I know the work, I know what they've got to do and I know how to motivate people usually, but I just think that they're impossible. They are very difficult to motivate and you know I just feel very unsupported in a way, and I feel that that's something that, that's why I thought I just must grab ten minutes to try and get this sorted out.

This is another rambling and emotional comment, which contains a criticism of Harry.

Harry Okay, perhaps we can start there and maybe talk about what it is you feel that I can do.

Harry changes approach. He asks what help he can give and so shows he has heard the criticism.

Cheryl Well, I think perhaps you could give me more support, I mean I hardly ever get to see you, I mean, I never see you, you're so busy. Whenever I ask your secretary if I can have five minutes with you, 'Oh no, no, he's much too busy, he can't be seen' You know, that's quite unsupportive really. Actually that I need time to see you. I just can't cope with this job, you know the way it's going, it's just impossible, the pressure of work as well has been increased – that's also a problem. Tremendous pressure to meet deadlines and, you know, it's very,very stressful.

This is a stronger criticism, but one which indicates a powerful need.

Harry Okay, so there are several issues that we need to talk about. One of them is the pressure of the workload and how you are dealing with the pressure of the workload and what that's meant to you, and also we need to review how the team is working and your relationship with the team. It also sounds like there is a further issue there and that's about our relationship and the kind of support and feedback that you're getting or not getting from me.

Harry lists the factual issues he has heard.

Cheryl I think that's right.

Harry So there are really three things we need to talk about. Now this afternoon, we have actually only booked ten minutes and we've used half of that up already. It sounds to me that we actually need a lot longer than five minutes in order to deal with that.

Harry decides the agenda is too long.

Cheryl Mmm.

Harry Erm, perhaps it would be a good idea right now if we booked some time, and I mean within the next day or so, to talk because it sounds like this is a very pressing problem.

And offers a more practical alternative.

Cheryl Mm. Well I'm really relieved to hear you say that really Harry because I just don't think, I just can't take any more really and I just needed to have some support.

Harry Okay, lets talk about the kind of support I can give you. I think we need to start with a little more discussing of what the situation is. When are you free tomorrow?

Cheryl Well, of course I've got a team meeting in the morning, and I'm seeing Josephine at eleven o'clock after that, and after that I'm seeing somebody, that buyer, is coming in from Yorkshire and then in the afternoon, I've got actually to have a planning meeting in the afternoon, but I've cancelled that.

Harry Yes, it sounds to me like this really over-rides just about everything except maybe outside suppliers so which of those, upon, let me just tell you, it would probably be more convenient for me, if we could use the morning so, erm ...

Cheryl Well I, you know, the way they're working at the moment. Frankly the team can meet just as well without me as with me, so I'll come in the morning.

Harry Okay and what are you going to say to your team about you not being at the meeting?

Cheryl Well, I'll say I've got an urgent meeting with you. They don't need to know what that's about, nothing to do with them really is it?

Harry No, that might be something we can talk about tomorrow perhaps. Okay lets leave that so that's, erm, 8.45 am tomorrow morning.

Cheryl Fine.

Harry Is that okay for you?

Cheryl Mm.

Harry Right, okay we'll meet at a quarter to nine tomorrow morning and I'll put aside an hour and we can talk about some of the things that you've raised.

Cheryl Thank you Harry.

Harry A pleasure.

Marginal notes:

Cheryl expresses relief and affirms her distress.

The rest of this interview is a friendly negotiation of terms for the next meeting.

Harry warns about a possible difficulty.

And confirms the venue and agenda and his own commitment.

Harry and Cheryl continued. Next day at 8.45 am Harry has decided he must hear Cheryl out and get a real understanding of her problems.

Cheryl Hello Harry.

Harry Hi Cheryl.

Cheryl Hi.

Harry Okay, great I'm glad we've got some time now to talk about some of the issues you raised yesterday. If I can just remind us about what sort of things you were saying yesterday. Some of the things you were talking about yesterday were ...

He sets the agenda.

we can really put it down to three major issues. One was how your team were working together, and your relationship with your team, and another issue was about the pressure of work and how you were dealing with the pressure of work. The third one was the relationship that you and I have and how little and how much support you felt that you were getting. Is that right?

Cheryl Yes, that sums it up quite well.

Harry Okay, I've made sure we won't be disturbed because I think it is very important that we talk this through without interruption so, the engaged light is on and the phone is being passed on somewhere else. Okay, so which one of those issues would you like to tackle first?

And promises privacy.

Cheryl Well, I think the one I first said when I saw you yesterday. By the way, I did feel a bit better having seen you yesterday, I was really at the end of my tether but the one that, around the staff and the calibre of staff that I am being given to work with really ...

Cheryl repeats her criticism but more indirectly and in friendlier fashion.

Harry Mmm.

Cheryl I mean, I'm, I really feel that I should be part of the selection interviewing but, erm, I know that you haven't wanted me to, but I really feel that I'm not there, so I'm actually just given the staff that you and, of course, Alan decide on and I feel that that's not actually right, but having said that, you know, I try and do the best I can with them.

This is a new version of the problem. She feels left out of decisions which affect her.

Harry It sounds to me that that does tie in with the other issue we mentioned about pressure of work. Maybe there is something about you; you say 'well I want to do the selection' and there is a limit to how much time each manager has and maybe there is something about the kind of staff we are selecting, erm, but that doesn't seem to have affected you in the past. As you say you have been here an awful long time. Thirteen years is a long time; you know the job and you also know that actually it is pure luck a lot of the time. If you actually get a great team, it's great and it's wonderful but it doesn't last for ever. So what is it about this team that you feel you can't handle.

Harry recognises this but sets it aside in favour of the agreed agenda.

Cheryl First of all, I think that they, you know, you seem to be going, and I don't know if this is a change in policy, the company, but you seem to be going for people with university degrees. Now it doesn't really help me that they've got a degree in history when I'm actually asking them to do a task which has nothing really to do and no relevance in terms of their degree, and you know that, that seems to have been some sort of decision has been made somewhere, which I've never been aware of, because my team have now all got some sort of degree education.

Her feeling of being left out is expressed more strongly, with a new cause.

Harry And that sounds like that makes you feel a little excluded.

He summarises the feeling her statement conveys.

Cheryl Well no, of course not, I've got the experience, I've been here 13 years and I've done the job and I'm very experienced and I know what I'm doing and I know they are very inexperienced and haven't got many skills. They've got an education but not many skills, I mean, that doesn't mean that, that's something I've been excluded from.

But she cannot quite acknowledge it yet.

Harry Well, that sounds like a rational explanation of what actually should happen but it doesn't sound like that's what's actually happening.

Harry points out the in consistency between her intellectual percep tion and her feelings.

Cheryl Oh no, but Harry, if I wanted to go to university I could have done but I actually chose not to. I did choose not to go to university and, you know, I think that was the right decision for me. Frankly, you know that I've always thought that in a few years time I'd do an Open University degree but, erm, it's not that, it's, I don't really feel that that's, not that important to me.

Cheryl still needs to justify herself.

Harry Well, it seems important to you that the fact that they're graduates so ...

He defines what he hears.

Cheryl Well, they're not really the right people for the job, that's what it is.

But she does not accept it.

Harry Tell me what it is about them as people that makes them wrong for the job.

Harry accepts her version and asks her to describe it more fully.

Cheryl Well, they've sort of got their heads in the clouds really. They're not very, they haven't got their feet on the ground, they've got their heads in the clouds and, erm, I think that's probably what happens to you when you go to university that it's, erm, a level of development that's completely different and it's difficult to get your feet on the ground.

She is happy to talk about this but her reply confirms that she does feel excluded.

Harry Perhaps you can give me some examples because I'm not quite sure what you mean when you say, 'head in the clouds' and 'feet on the ground'. Perhaps you can give me some examples where that kind of behaviour actually disrupts, because that's what you're saying.

Harry asks for examples of her difficulty.

Cheryl Well, erm of course, I can give you hundreds of examples. Yesterday, before I came to see you we had a team meeting. We were looking at trying to get the product, erm, out, and instead of being able to actually look at the breaking down of how we were actually going to go about it, we were ending up in some sort of, erm, high falutin' discussion about the ethics of the product. You know that's not really what I feel is relevant to the job and it's very interesting if that's what they want to do, but it's not the point. I want to get on with the task, and the task is to get the product out.

The example vividly il luminates Cheryl's iso lation.

Harry Mm, that sounds quite appropriate that your role is to make sure that the team get the product out and that sounds as though it's right. Perhaps you could tell me exactly, what did you do when they began this discussion about the ethics of the product?

Harry accepts her de finition of her respons bilities and encourages her to de scribe the situation fu ther.

Cheryl Well, I listened for a moment or two, and then I realised that they were having a completely, ridiculous conversation so I told them that, that they were to stop immediately and to continue focusing on what we are supposed to be doing. Well, of course they didn't like that and then they all start, erm, horsing around. You see, that's another example I'd like to give you is the sort of horsing around and horse-play that goes on, you know, when I try to, erm, get some sort of control, over them they all start to be very clever and joke around and horse about, and that's very difficult to control, so I lost my temper and I started shouting at them.

Harry Mm, and how did that feel for you when you lost your temper?

Cheryl Well, I don't like losing my temper at the best of times really and it didn't really do any good because it carried on.

Harry Why do you think they carried on when you lost your temper?

Cheryl I don't know. It was very upsetting actually.

Harry Mm, it must have been very upsetting for you because you were in a situation where you felt, 'I don't know what's going on here, why won't they do as I say?' And they appear to be ignoring you, and that actually sounds as though that's something that you feel a lot of the time, not just when you lose your temper, but actually you feel that they don't listen to you.

Cheryl Well, you see I think what they don't ... I think you're right, they don't listen to me and they don't seem to appreciate that I've been here a long time and I do know what I'm talking about, and I do have some experience and skills. They don't seem to be able to see that really.

Harry Have you told them about, I mean, you have got a great wealth of experience and skills here. How do they know about your experience and skills?

Cheryl Well, I don't like to shove it down their throats really.

Harry Mmm, yes.

Cheryl And of course I don't know, I mean I don't know, I wouldn't tell them because I wouldn't, erm, I think that would be shoving it down their throats.

Harry I was just wondering whether they are not aware of your skills and experience and so the only bit that they're seeing is, actually you perhaps, erm, telling them to do things without understanding why you are telling them that; why you feel that that's the right way to go; I mean you've worked all that through in your head, and you know from experience and knowledge, that that's probably the most appropriate way to do it, but they may not know that.

She elaborates what happened. The conflicts with her team become clearer.

She admits she mishandled the situation.

Harry does not comment on this, but summarises what she has told him.

This time Cheryl can admit more of her feelings although she still needs self-justification.

Harry's suggestion sounds difficult to put into practice.

And Cheryl finds it so.

He rephrases it and uses the opportunity to reassure her.

Cheryl So what do you think I should do? Send out a newsletter about my experience and skills. I mean how do I go about telling them?

Harry Well, let's take the example that you said yesterday about a new product going out. It sounded, and I may have got this wrong, but it sounded to me like you were having a discussion about, about how a product went out. Now you've been doing this for a long time, you know the ins and outs and the kind of things that need to be done now. I'm sure, of course, it's possible that there may be extra additions that other people could make, I mean that's the way life goes on, it changes and we get new ideas, erm, but all the same we need to build on something that's strong and that's got a track record which you have.

Cheryl I'll have to tell you Harry, and this is a point I'm really highlighting for myself, if they haven't, they can't really help this, that way; they haven't really got anything that is constructive so I don't listen to them most of the time because they are stupid, they come up with stupid suggestions.

Harry Well let's hang on a second there, there are two things coming up now. One of them is how you get across to them that you actually have a point to make. The other thing is that how they get across to you that they may have a contribution to make. It sounds to me that you think they have no contribution to make.

Cheryl Not much really.

Harry And on what are you basing that judgement?

Cheryl On the experience of them.

Harry But what chance have you given them to make a contribution?

Cheryl They come to meetings. They have the chance of speaking.

Harry What kind of chance do they ... in what sort of way do they have a chance of making a contribution?

Cheryl I ask them what they think.

Harry About?

Cheryl Anything I might be making a decision on. But most of the time, they haven't got a relevant point to make, so I make the decision on my own and I just tell them that's what the decision is. Because I do think you have to have control of your department really.

Harry I'm just wondering about what you've just said because what I heard in that was something about, erm, you having made the decision before you went to the meeting.

Cheryl Well, don't all managers do that?

Harry Sometimes it's necessary for a manager to make a decision and say this is the decision and that's it. There are other times though when a manager really does want the contributions of his staff or her staff. You're looking for a contribution from the staff and therefore you invite their contributions. Now, I feel quite strongly that actually, if you really want a contribution from them, then you must listen to what they say.

He acknowledges that her style can be appropriate at times but suggests it will not help her team to respond constructively.

Cheryl Well you see, that's where we differ because I don't really want a contribution from them, I want you to get me better staff who can have a contribution to make.

Cheryl reacts defensively again.

Harry That's two separate things though; one is I don't want a contribution from them and the other one is I want better staff.

And Harry again points out her inconsistency.

Cheryl All I'm saying is, when they contribute they haven't got anything valuable to say, so I think we come back to the first point; if we got better type, better staff they ... I would want to listen to their contribution.

Cheryl nevertheless persists that this is how she sees things.

Harry I think we are back to the other issue about how you feel about your staff aren't we, and I think this is something separate. This is about you assessing what's good and bad in members of staff.

Harry tries to clarify the different points she is raising.

Cheryl Yes.

Harry And what you feel you need. Let me just pull together something, because I actually get the impression that we're walking round the issue at the moment, and we're sort of touching on peripheral symptoms if you like, but we're not actually getting to the heart of the matter. Erm, and a couple of things you've said made me feel that, and again touching on one of the other issues about pressure and control, those two words seem to figure very strongly in some of the things you are saying, erm, and I'm wondering if there isn't something, a nub at the heart of this, that, yes, these are all issues that you are dealing with, but they are not at the heart of the matter. Have I got that right?

Harry abandons confrontation and tries stating his own confusion.

He shows that he has begun to accept that some other issue has to be faced.

Cheryl I don't know, what do you think is, you tell me what you think is at the heart of the matter, and I'll be able to say if you've go it right.

Cheryl is cautious. She wants him to define what the issue may be.

Harry Well I don't know, that's why I'm asking you. But the fact that you answered it in that way would imply to me that actually you feel that there is something more fundamental, because you say that you will know if I've got it right, so is there something very fundamental that's actually bugging you at the moment?

But Harry keeps his reply general while confirming his feeling that there is another and bigger issue.

Cheryl Well if you put it like that, I suppose one of the things that I am feeling a bit sort of cross about is the change in policy that I am witnessing in the company, where people with a university qualification are coming in and I have been here 13 years and have done my time, and I'm only a unit manager these 13 years later, and I actually can see that the young up-

And this time Cheryl is more accepting. Even so, she seems only able to repeat what has troubled her before.

starts are going to be rushing in and have got the right words and the right presence and will soon be appointed well beyond me.

Harry So what you're saying in that is you feel that we don't value your skills and experience as much as we value those of these new people that are coming in.

Harry reflects this.

Cheryl I think that's, I think you've just hit the nail on the head Harry.

And gains her agreement.

Harry That's right.

Cheryl And I certainly think that comes from you as well. I mean, I find that that's very much from you, because you have been the appointing person in these interviews, and it's you that has changed the policy of the company, and never before have we had such so many graduates in the company before.

Cheryl is at last able to approach the main issue and complain more specifically about Harry's own behaviour.

Harry Tell me what it is that you feel about graduates that is not appropriate?

He chooses to encourage her to explore her specific concern over graduates.

Cheryl Well as I said to you, they've got their head in their cloud, got their heads in the clouds and not their feet on the ground, and the task of the manager is to bring them down and put their feet on the ground.

She only repeats what she has said before.

Harry Hang on a second, I don't want to get lost in that argument because that's going backwards to where we were before and I thought we were actually progressing to the heart of the matter. I've got a very strong feeling actually that, that, and I did mention it earlier, erm, that I sense that you feel very threatened by the graduates or by the people who are working for you right now.

Harry directs her away from repetition of criticism and back to what he hears of her real feelings.

Cheryl Threatened? I suppose if you put it like that, erm, I don't know actually, what do you mean?

Harry Well, what do you think that they can do to you?

Cheryl Well, they, they are going, I, I suppose what I've just said is what I fear, is that they are actually going to overtake me.

This time she expresses a serious fear.

Harry Right, so, the theory is that promotion in the organisation is now going to be revolving around what people's academic qualifications are rather than their abilities.

Harry states her fear explicitly.

Cheryl Yes.

Harry That certainly isn't the intention of the company but something is obviously making you feel like that, and I wonder whether there was an incident that has happened that has made you feel like that.

He reassures her but asks her to talk about it.

Cheryl Well, I, I don't think there's one incident. I think it's just a feeling I've been getting within the new appointments for all graduates, with your difficulty of actually making time to see me, with people rushing around and, erm, not feeling that they want to spend much time even with the people ...

And she reiterates her sense of being alone and left behind.

my peers, my colleagues don't spend much time with me and just a feeling that I was being isolated and that I must ... I belong to yesterday's man.

Harry Mm, that does sound like a feeling that you are somewhere over here on one side, and everybody else is rushing along and you're just watching them go past. That's the sort of picture I'm getting. I'm wondering if actually there isn't ... one of the things that I think is possibly happening is the fact that, because that's something you fear, that actually you are creating an environment where it could actually happen, because we have had no complaint with your work all the time that you've been here, quite the reverse, we've put people with you, we want them to actually see how things are done and that's why we put new recruits with you, erm, I mean that's, that's ...

Harry relates the problem as he now hears it and goes on to strong reassurance.

Cheryl Mm, yes.

Harry That's true and I know ...

Cheryl I like that actually, I like having new recruits, being able to show them the ropes.

They are able to agree an area where Cheryl's expertise is particularly valued.

Harry Yes, and you show them the ropes and they actually go on from that, and they couldn't go on without a solid foundation.

Cheryl's next remark gives extra insight into her resentment.

Cheryl Mm.

Harry What I think is happening, is that you are actually beginning to resent the fact that you're showing them the ropes, and they are actually moving on and you're not.

Harry shows he has heard this by his accurate reflection.

Cheryl I, yes, I think, I think that's right actually, I think that's very right, I think that's how I am feeling.

Which she accepts.

Harry You see what we have to ... and that in its turn having an effect on how you deal with them because obviously if you resent somebody then it's very difficult to actually deal with them in an objective way, erm, and I think perhaps what we have to look at is actually, what is actually happening and whether it may not be appropriate for you to be working with a particular group.

This remark of Harry's is highly confusing as though he were struggling himself to sort out where they are heading. He makes a clumsy suggestion.

Cheryl Well, what work would you give me to do if you didn't have me working with them?

And Cheryl feels threatened again.

Harry Well, what I am saying now is, I think we need to understand better what the situation really is and whether it's a real problem, or whether it's something that's going through your head right now, and maybe us talking it through might even relieve you of it. For example, you mentioned several times that you feel that I don't support you enough and I am wondering if we can actually do something with that, that would actually make you feel that actually you were valued because it ... the other thing I feel very strongly is that, not only do you feel threatened by the graduates, but you feel,

Harry at last recognises that he himself may have a part to play in the solution.

you don't feel valued by your manager, erm, and so there is some work that has to be done by me as well; actually letting you know how I feel about that.

Cheryl Mm, well, what I feel is I think you are right in what you are saying, but it's very worrying for me, because I've worked for this company for the last 13 years, I came from working down the road with W S Grahams and before that I worked with another firm in the same line of work, and now I am 47 years of age, it's not going to be that easy for me to go and find myself another job, and I like working for this firm but I feel that I'm not, there's something ... I'm not feeling that you want me working here any more.

Perhaps it is his greater involvement that enables Cheryl to respond with more of her worries.

Harry So there is quite a lot of work that I need to do, and we need to talk about what it is that you feel I don't want, erm, because there are several things here. What I certainly don't want, and lets have this out, what I don't want is you feeling unhappy and your team feeling unhappy because that isn't going to get the product out.

Harry continues to recognise what he must do and stresses that he wants to help her.

Cheryl Oh, I agree, I agree and that's why I came to you.

Harry I also understand that for you ... you take a lot of pride in your work and actually getting the product out on time and in the best possible way has actually been a standard you've set yourself and have achieved over the last 13 years. There's no way I want that disrupted, either from a personal point of view or from the company's point of view.

And acknowledges her skills again.

Cheryl Well, you know it's very nice to hear you say this, but it's a shame I've had to, erm, I've not heard you say it before, and I've had to come to this point in the situation where I've actually ... am at breaking point really, to hear you say it.

In this attack, Cheryl indicates the real problem for her is her relationship with Harry.

Harry I think you're right. I think that I have actually been taking the work, the good work, that you've done, for granted and just accepted it as it is, and there may be something in that that we can use. I need now to actually say, start thinking about the relationship which I've taken for granted, because you do your job so well, but there's something about that that we need to take down to you and your staff as well.

Harry now accepts this and accepts his own responsibility for improving matters.

Cheryl Mm, yes.

Harry Something about taking them for granted and/or making misinterpretations of what they can and can't do and perhaps that's one way of actually working with the situation – that if you see them in sort of parallel maybe we can do some work that way... .

Cheryl Well, that would be very good.

2. Jeremy's 'mid-life crisis'

Interview between Jeremy, a senior manager, and his boss, Ella

Jeremy is a 44 year old senior manager who was recently appraised by his boss, Ella Saunders. They have a good working relationship and mutual respect for each others' competence.

Jeremy is a specialist at the top of his promotional ladder and could advance only by leaving to find another job outside the company. This would almost certainly mean relocation. Hitherto it has suited him to stay; he has a delightful home; his work is interesting and he is well paid.

However, there is no doubt that whilst still working competently, Jeremy has gradually lost enthusiasm and he does not quite know why. At his appraisal, Ella and Jeremy agreed lack of enthusiasm was the main difficulty they could identify in what had otherwise been, from the company's point of view, a satisfactory year. They further agreed to meet again in an attempt to discover the source of Jeremy's disaffection. Ella has heard rumours that Jeremy's marriage is not going well, though he has not raised the matter. She has met his wife on official occasions and found her charming. Jeremy has mentioned how capable she is.

Ella has decided to conduct this second meeting as a counselling interview, concentrating on understanding Jeremy and so, she hopes, helping him to understand himself.

Although the background and names are disguised, this is otherwise an exact transcript of their conversation.

Ella Last week when we had our appraisal, we were doing your appraisal, we talked at some length about what's gone on over the past year. It seemed to both of us that actually you weren't quite sure what you wanted, or where you wanted to go from here, so we agreed that you would go away, and come back this week when you had time to think about what was going on, and what you wanted. So today we have got an hour where we can discuss where you want to go, and any issues you want to talk about. Does that sound okay to you?

Although inconclusive, the previous session had ended positively with a plan to meet to discuss a particular issue. Jeremy has had a week to think things over. Ella sets the objective of the second meeting and gives the time limit at the outset.

Jeremy That's fine.

Ella Okay. Perhaps you would like to start by telling me some of the things you have been thinking about over the past week.

Jeremy Well Ella, I have been thinking about what you said, about what you said last week, thinking about it all weekend, still none the wiser really. I'm really not sure where I want to go from here. I've been thinking I'm bored where I am at the moment. I'm not sure what direction I want to take, there's things going on in my personal life as well, so I'm not clear. I can't really come back to you now and say this is what I want to do or thought about.

Ella Okay – well, there is a couple of things there that you mentioned. One of the things was, you said you were bored with work and the other thing was that there were a couple of things in your personal life. Let's take the issues about work first. Let's talk about these things – you said you were bored with work. What exactly do you mean by, you were bored at work?

Jeremy still seems vague but Ella finds two areas where they may be able to make progress. She suggests talking first about work, the 'safer' area.

Jeremy Well, I have done the same job for the last ten years, but I think I've mastered it; I've got it under my belt and there's not much challenge for me any more. Some days quite honestly, I am having to work and I don't know what I'm coming in there for and do it. I'm not excited, I'm not challenged.

Ella And how long do you think you've been feeling like this?

Ella ascertains the size of the problem.

Jeremy Hard to say, probably a couple of years.

Ella A couple of years?

This is rather surprising; the problem was not identified in Jeremy's appraisal last year.

Jeremy I wouldn't be surprised. Now I think about it I've not been conscious of it. If you ask me, I'll say a couple of years.

Ella That's how you think you're feeling. What sort of effect do you think that's had on your work?

Jeremy I've just lacked enthusiasm. I've probably been a bit lapse. I've heard it all before and, erm, lacked an energy and drive. Those are the main symptoms.

Jeremy acknowledges some reduction in effort which his uncertainties have brought on.

Ella That's you talking about it. Now, are those things that you can think about, looking back on how you've been over the last few years or so, or are they things you've actually noticed?

Ella tries to discover if Jeremy is reporting feelings or perceived performance.

Jeremy Well not things I have noticed until recently, and nothing very specific, but now you are bringing it to my attention, I can certainly see little things, letting little things slip, well I can trace them back for two years or more.

Ella Let's try and tie it down a bit, and talk about whether it's actually to do with the job, or whether it's to do with the organisation. So what I'm saying is, is it actually to do with the work you're doing, or have other things been happening?

Jeremy's work has not suffered. Ella tries to get a full picture of his present feelings.

Jeremy Well I suppose there had been some changes in the organisation. I've not really had any promotion out of these changes and there isn't any chance of that, so that is a factor as well. I suppose I feel some resentment about that even though I've decided, well you know on balance I've decided to accept it. It's the content of the work I've always enjoyed and that's not changed. *I* have. I think that is the most serious factor.

Jeremy considers this wider perspective but accepts that the change is in himself.

Ella So the thing that really is at the heart of it, or maybe the most important item is, the fact that you feel you can do the work. You know you can do the work. But you've lost interest. There is nothing new for you. Is that it?

Ella summarises what she has heard so far, to make sure they are agreed.

Jeremy I should really have a change and I can't think what I really can do within the organisation or, to be honest, outside it.

Jeremy admits to some despair; this is a bigger admission than anything he has said so far.

Ella What you have just said now is you said that 'I should really have a change'. What do you mean by 'I should'?

Ella picks up the word 'should' which is more about duty than desire. It may give her a better understanding of the pressure Jeremy feels.

Jeremy Well I put that forward as one possible solution. If I am doing the same thing for too long and I have no enthusiasm for it, or finding it a bit purposeless, perhaps I should change.

Ella I am just trying to sort out for myself and for you, what exactly it is that makes you want to change.

She encourages Jeremy to try to define his own motivation.

Jeremy Well maybe I'm not being very positive about it. What I am saying is, I am unhappy doing what I'm doing. I'm stuck doing what I am doing, therefore perhaps I need a change.

He cannot yet do this.

Ella So you feel stuck but you're not sure why you feel stuck.

So Ella picks up another word; exploring what this means may help.

Jeremy Not sure why I feel stuck or where I want to go.

Ella And one of the things you're suggesting might help to unstick you is to actually change.

Jeremy I think that might, yes.

Ella One of the things that would concern you about that, would be not understanding why you feel stuck, because the same issue might arise again, mightn't it? If we change your job for example, if we weren't sure exactly what it was that was making you feel stuck.

Ella points out that Jeremy's 'solution' may not be based on understanding the problem.

Jeremy Would it not just be that I am bored and I have been doing the same thing that I have mastered? There's no challenge left.

He claims it is a reasonable assumption.

Ella Yes, it could well be that, it could well be that. What interests me about that is, lets talk about that for a bit. And this bit about 'there's no challenge left'. You mentioned that you'd felt like this for two years. What is it that actually is, actually is bringing things to a head right now.

Accepting this, Ella tries the word 'challenge' and reminds Jeremy that their present meeting has significance. Why are they meeting now?

Jeremy It's difficult to put a finger on it. Probably the appraisal you did with me last week brought things to a head. As I said, there's things going on outside my life as well which maybe are making, bringing things to a head generally.

Ella has waited for Jeremy to initiate any talk of personal issues. This remark shows he is ready to do so.

Ella Maybe its an appropriate time to bring those issues in and talk about some of those personal issues. Perhaps you could tell me a bit about those?

Jeremy Well to be honest, my marriage is going through a bit of a rocky time at the moment, the kids are growing up, I have had a relationship which has been quite important to me, but it's certainly not a relationship I feel completely balanced about, and I think that this has stirred me up and certainly has affected me at work.

Ella Do you feel that the need to have a relationship and erm the kids growing up, do you feel those two are related in any way?

Jeremy Possibly, possibly. There's a sense of things are changing, certainly it's been in my wife. I think it's affected her probably more than me or the kids leaving home, and through its affecting her, it's affected my relationship with her, which I suppose again, if I looked back on it, it hasn't just begun with the kids leaving, it's been going on for some time, and then I met Prue and she came I suppose, at a time when I was ready to have a relationship, give me some purpose in life.

Ella And what sort of stage is that relationship at right now?

Jeremy We have been seeing each other for a couple of years now.

Ella For a couple of years?

Jeremy Well I suppose it's become more intense and she's beginning to make demands on me too about leaving my wife.

Ella And how do you feel about her making demands on you?

Jeremy I'm not sure really to commit myself to actually leave her, leave my wife, go and live with Prue. I'm still not sure about that.

Ella Well, that sounds as though that might have quite an effect on your work, if you have this decision to make outside your work, which is a very important decision for you, about whether you stay with your wife or go with Prue. That sounds to me like it would be having quite a lot of influence on the way you behave at work.

Jeremy Yes, it could be.

Ella What sort of things do you think it might affect?

She acknowledges the change.

This is an important admission which Ella must receive neutrally.

She uses his own words and suggests he explore the connections.

Jeremy becomes more open about his situation. His response indicates that he is prepared to continue to discuss it.

Ella notes that Jeremy's work unhappiness coincides with his finding a new partner, but stops short of making any explicit connection.

Ella is still careful to use Jeremy's own words to help him explore his situation.

She risks suggesting that this is an important difficulty which must be affecting him at work.

She encourages him to define its effects.

Jeremy I suppose it makes me, my, at times a little distracted because I worry about it. I wouldn't say it's affecting ... you did the evaluation on me last week. I wouldn't say it's affected drastically my performance. I think I have high standards for myself and I would be dishonest if I said it didn't have some effect.

Ella I seem to remember from what you said last week, it's not the work per se, more your dealing with the rest of your staff.

Jeremy Yes I have been irritable with my staff, I mean I've been short with them, partly because, as I said, I'm bored and partly because I'm distracted.

Ella We've talked a bit about work and we've talked a bit about the relationship you're having and right now I get the feeling that there are an awful lot of question marks both over your work and your personal life. Have I got that right?

Ella gives another summary. Coming from another person it may serve to clarify and highlight the main issues in Jeremy's situation.

Jeremy Yes, that's a fair assessment.

Ella And I guess that the question that we have to look at is actually 'where do we go from here in dealing with those question marks'.

She suggests they look for practical solutions.

Jeremy Yes, as I said to you, I really don't know the answer.

But Jeremy cannot make this step yet.

Ella When I actually ask you these questions what sort of feelings do you have about where you go from here?

Ella recognises he has to talk more about his feelings.

Jeremy I suppose I feel a bit hopeless really.

Ella Hopeless? In what way do you feel hopeless?

Jeremy Well I thought these things through and I feel very stuck; the work problems have been going on a long time and, besides, my relationship and my marital problems have been going on a long time and I can't see any solution. I feel a bit stuck and hopeless really.

He repeats the words he used earlier.

Ella That's a word you have used several times in this conversation – stuck. And it strikes me that we need actually to find something which will commence an unsticking as it were. Before we can actually, before we do move you on forward there needs to be some unsticking.

She accepts his feeling but shows she does not accept that no change is possible.

Jeremy That would be most welcome.

Ella My first thought about that is that actually you need a bit more space than the kind of time that we have in the appraisal and, because some of your problems are very personal problems, my feeling would be that we actually need an environment that perhaps isn't a working environment, that's perhaps with somebody who you feel you could talk through in a lot more depth those which you have touched on with me.

She risks putting a possible course of action which might help him.

Jeremy Look, I appreciate your concern with me, but I don't think I have got any more serious problems than maybe a lot of other people have. At my age and at my career stage if you're suggesting that I get some sort of therapy, I don't think I am the sort of person that would benefit from it. I'm not sure that is the right thing for me. I'm being frank with you and I'm telling you how I feel. You're trying to solve my problem at work but I'm not sure that seeing somebody outside would warrant it.

But again it has come too early. Jeremy resists the proposal quite strongly.

Ella I think there are a couple of things there, things that I would like to pick up. One of them is that I don't ... I'm not suggesting that maybe you going into therapy would be an answer for you. I'm wondering whether actually you and I talking together would be an appropriate place to discuss the issues that you brought.

Ella's response is to disclose something of her own predicament.

Jeremy Well I just wanted you to be in the picture. I've been honest with you.

Jeremy points out indirectly that she has invited this situation.

Ella Yes now I understand that. I think it's, I think I feel it's something more to do with actually not much I can do with the information you have given me, and how much we can do with what you have told me.

Ella accepts this and gives an honest account of her own feelings.

Jeremy Yes I see that.

Ella And therefore whether that is something we can deal with, you know, maybe in this office, or whether it is something which perhaps you need just a bit of extra time with somebody else, to try to get a perspective on the issues you have raised, and then come back.

She justifies her proposal accordingly.

Jeremy Yes I see. I just have a reluctance ... I'm not the sort of person who is going to go looking for help in that way.

And Jeremy becomes less antagonistic to the idea.

Ella Right I understand that, erm, I think also that I hear that some of you, part of you actually feels as though that you do need to talk to somebody else.

Ella must recognise this change very tentatively at this stage.

Jeremy Yes, but it goes against the grain.

Ella Let me, let me just ask you something about going against the grain. What is it that worries you about going against the grain?

She decides to encourage him to explore his resistance.

Jeremy It's hard to put a finger on it. I've never done it before, never asked anybody for help. I'm not that sort of person. I don't talk about my feelings. Look, I've not thought about this before, as I said, it's not the way I normally respond to a problem but, as you point out, it is affecting my work.

He gives an honest reply which has implications for the whole situation he is facing.

Ella There's also ...

Jeremy And I haven't seen that before. Maybe I need to think about it, what you're suggesting.

This is his first constructive response.

Ella Yes I think that something you said about, not, well several times you've repeated, it's not something you've come across before. And ...

Jeremy That's true.

Ella Erm, maybe new issues demand new solutions, and maybe because this is a situation you've not found yourself in before, it may require you to do something that you haven't done before in order to deal with it.

Ella picks up the new situation.

Jeremy Yes, perhaps you are right. I'd have to think about it more.

This important advance owes much to Ella's redefinition of her proposal in terms of her needs as well as Jeremy's.

Ella That sounds reasonable. As I say it is something new, erm, I am quite aware that we are having a conversation which is, that's interesting and I'd like to go away and think about it and I feel that we do have to say that, erm, we must come to some kind of pragmatic sort of answer at the end, erm though that may not be today, but I would like to arrange to have a brief talk with you about this tomorrow.

Ella decides that both she and Jeremy are now working actively on the problem and need a short respite.

She stipulates that it must be brief.

Jeremy Tomorrow?

Ella Mm, yes, I'd like to do it tomorrow.

Jeremy Okay.

Ella What was your hesitation then for tomorrow?

Jeremy I thought you might give me a week.

Jeremy's response shows he is still rather scared of what he has admitted.

Ella Erm, I don't think so, I think we have had a week in between one and the other and I think this is far more important maybe for us to actually get a start on this.

Ella is confident enough to impose this condition.

Jeremy Okay.

Ella Perhaps if you feel that you want more time I'd like to know exactly things you'd need more time for.

But offers him more time, on specific terms.

Jeremy Well I expect you're right. I don't think there's much point in delaying it. I will think about what you said and I'll speak to you about it tomorrow.

He then accepts her condition.

Ella Okay. So we've discussed several issues about you, and where you are at the moment right now and what we're agreeing now, is that you'll consider the ideas that I've put to you about maybe talking some of your more personal issues through with somebody else?

She reminds him of the proposal he has to consider.

Jeremy Who have you got in mind?

Jeremy still seems prepared to resist the idea.

Ella Well I think I'd like to, should we discuss that further tomorrow, and because I'd like to hear your thoughts about it about the process of the whole, rather than, if you like, the details and I have nobody in mind at this current moment in

If Ella replies precisely, she will meet more resistance. She therefore simply acknowledges

time. Er, I think I perhaps need to think about it as well. Does that make sense to you?

that they both have work to do.

Jeremy Yes

Ella Okay, so tomorrow, erm, let's, can you make three o' clock?

The appointment time sets a target for them to work to.

Jeremy Yes, I can.

Ella Okay, perhaps if we can put aside half an hour tomorrow and discuss this some more.

And he knows well in advance how long he has for the meeting.

Jeremy Okay.

Ella Okay, thanks very much.

A courtesy phrase which nevertheless concludes the meeting warmly.

Appendix III

Questionnaire: Are You a Potential Counsellor?

■ Self assessment Questionnaire

Try yourself out on these six cases. All have been calculated from the observations and recordings from real work situations. You may find them all t familiar.

You do not need to know the speaker's background or circumstances to write down your reactions and what you might say to someone telling you thes things. Ask someone else to do the same, preferably someone whose counselling skills you respect. Then discuss your different approaches and decide between you what response (yours, theirs, another you jointly devise) would best encourage the speaker to respond as constructively as possible.

You could also decide what response would encourage them to respond a: destructively as possible. To build constructive situations it is often helpful to consider how they are destroyed as well as how they are built up. Complete th self scoring in the light of your discussions and after comparing your suggestions with your colleague's and your agreed 'ideal'.

1. William hates this meeting

William talks to a friend after a meeting. He says:

'Thank God that's over. I hate those meetings. Everyone keeps telling everybody else how brilliant they are with chapter and verse. That's all it's for really. I find it awful. I simply can't think of anything I've done ever and so I just clam up. Then when it's all over and I remember I've done this, that and the other and it's pretty good. It's certainly at least as good as anything they were all talking about. Why couldn't I say so?'

What would you say to help William sort out his situation? Why?

What I would say	Why?	How I think William would respond
What A N Other would say	Why?	How do they think William would respond
What might be an ideal response	Why?	How might William respond

Self scoring

I assess my original statement as likely to produce a reaction which would be:

Destructive	Quite negative	Neutral	Quite positive	Constructive

Reasons for your assessment:

2. Clara feels let down

Clara describes an aspect of a recent office move:

'When Anna left it was like seeing a house of cards come down. We were discussing the move and I knew if Anna came everyone else would. We needed them all to carry out the move successfully. She took a long, long time to decide and then told me she was resigning. I knew that meant half the staff would go because they very much looked to her and the advantages and disadvantages were otherwise much the same for them. She knew it too. I felt very betrayed. Perhaps I just trust people too much.'

What would you say to help Clara analyse her situation constructively?

What I would say	Why?	How I think Clara would respond
What A N Other would say	Why?	How do they think Clara would respond
What might be an ideal response	Why?	How might Clara respond

Self scoring

I assess my original response as likely to produce from Clara a reaction which would be:

Destructive	Quite negative	Neutral	Quite positive	Constructive

Reasons for your assesment:

3. Julienne talks about anger

Describing a recent work situation, Julienne says:

> 'When she missed the deadline I felt furious. I had been warning her for weeks. I called her in and told her how I felt. She just said that she had no idea I felt so strongly. I was annoyed.
>
> I've always been told I always appear very controlled. I do tell people when I'm angry. I say, 'what you have done has these various effects and puts me in such and such a position and I feel extremely angry'. But I think it's quite wrong to behave at work as I usually would if I were angry at home. I mean, I don't storm about and throw things or yell my head off. I think showing your real feelings would be totally wrong at work.'

What would you say to help Julienne discover more constructive ways of expressing her anger?

What I would say	Why?	How I think Julienne would respond
What A N Other would say	Why?	How do they think Julienne would respond
What might be an ideal response	Why?	How might Julienne respond

Self scoring

I assess my original response as likely to produce from Julienne a reaction which would be:

Destructive	Quite negative	Neutral	Quite positive	Constructive

Reasons for your assessment:

4. Edward's relocation

Edward relocated six months ago and now expresses his mixed feelings.

'Well, it's a charming little town and everyone in the new office is friendly, though I've noticed that doesn't extend to social life. Everyone leaves at 5.30 pm and that's the last we see of each other until next morning. The office itself? Well, it's small – really very small. Twenty people or so but the offices themselves are tiny. I could play footy-footy with my secretary but she's not my type.

And they do a lot of things in a daft way. Well, it may make sense but it's different from what I'm used to and I haven't seen the point of much of it so far. I could ask to go back to Headquarters. It would mean goodbye to any advancement but Mary and I would probably be happier. As things are we only meet every other weekend.'

What might you say to Edward to help him analyse his situation and why he is feeling the way he does?

What I would say	Why?	How I think Edward would respond
What A N Other would say	Why?	How do they think Edward would respond
What might be an ideal response	Why?	How might Edward respond

Self scoring

I assess my original response as likely to produce from Edward a reaction which would be:

Destructive	Quite negative	Neutral	Quite positive	Constructive

Reasons for your assessment:

5. Alden queries his new boss

Alden's new boss came in a year ago on his predecessor's retirement. Alden's assessment is:

'I can see why higher management like him. He writes all sorts of no doubt brilliant reports and he's always off to meet them all and to attend this, that and the other function. All very good stuff, no doubt, no, I mean that. Means this department gets noticed and he does too of course.

Then there's this new proposal he's just sent around about reorganising the department, which it certainly needs. I've had a quick look at it and it will iron out one or two snags. But it won't get to the bottom of our problems.

It's the same old story. Last year I wrote a report on reorganisation for Peters, his predecessor. God knows where that went; I never heard another word about it. Well, we'll see, I've one or two alternative futures for myself if I can't see things working out here.'

What might you say to Alden to help him understand his ambivalent feelings about his boss and the company.

What I would say	Why?	How I think Alden would respond
What A N Other would say	Why?	How do they think Alden would respond
What might be an ideal response	Why?	How might Alden respond

Self scoring

I assess my original response as likely to produce from Alden a reaction which would be:

Destructive	Quite negative	Neutral	Quite positive	Constructive

Reasons for your assessment:

6. Jock has a major work load

Jock would manage well with a 36-hour day. He says:

'It's all interesting and worthwhile, I'm not disputing that. It's just over-whelming. I no sooner clear one project than six more turn up, all as im-portant as each other. We could do with three of us in the office and it would be very well worth the firm's while to employ us all on double my salary – as I keep telling everyone. They think it's a bit of a laugh, be-cause, as we all know, in fact there's a very tight constraint on recruiting, especially at my level.

Carew says one should cut corners and that's how he keeps his week ends clear but I can't do that. I work pretty fast but one has to be thor-ough, I think. If I get it wrong it could cost us or the client a real packet. I do take work home but that doesn't make for happiness. Betty's getting fed up and even the kids complain.'

What might you say to Jock to help him constructively analyse his attitude to work and his need to 'prove' his worth.

What I would say	Why?	How I think Jock would respond
What A N Other would say	Why?	How do they think Jock would respond
What might be an ideal response	Why?	How might Jock respond

Self scoring

I assess my original response as likely to produce from Jock a reaction which would be:

Destructive	Quite negative	Neutral	Quite positive	Constructive

Reasons for your assessment:

Appendix IV

Training in Counselling

This is a list of some of the many organisations providing training for counsellors. There are many more in provincial locations. For a full list, see the British Association of Counselling Training Directory.

Alcohol Counselling Service
  34 Electric Lane
  London SW9 8JT

Association of Independent Psycho-
  therapists
  P O Box 1194
  London N6 5PW
  Venue: North London

British Association of Psychotherapists
  21 Hendon Lane
  London N3 3PR

CEPEC
  Kent House
  41 East Street
  Bromley
  Kent BR11 1QQ
  *Training for personnel managers, wel-
  fare, career and management development training. Setting up
  counselling services in organisations. Redundancy counselling. Pub-
  lications.*

Dr Sandra Delroy
  Chartered Clinical Psychologist
  3 Northumberland House
  237 Ballards Lane
  Finchley
  London N3 1LB

Family Planning Association
  Education Unit
  27-35 Mortimer Street
  London W1N 7RJ

Lincoln Centre and Institute for
  Psychotherapy
  19 Abbeville Mews
  88 Clapham Park Road
  London SW4 7BX

London University – Birkbeck College
  Centre for Extra-Mural Studies
  26 Russell Square
  London WC1 5DQ

Westminster Pastoral Foundation
  23 Kensington Square
  London W8 5HN

Appendix V

Where to Get Counselling

This is a list of some of the many organisations that provide a counselling service.

Ashley Associates
  6 Lower Sloane Street
  London SW1W 8BJ
  Stress counselling – deals with addiction, smoking, alcohol, neuroses.

Independent Counselling and Advisory
  Services
  P O Box 615
  Woburn Sands
  Milton Keynes NK17 87W
  All aspects of counselling.

British Association of Counselling
  37a Sheep Street
  Rugby CV21 3BX
  Central Information.

British Association of Psychotherapists
  121 Hendon Lane
  London N3 3P3
  081-346 1747
  Referral and assessment services.

Pauline Hyde and Associates
  20 Lincoln's Inn Fields
  London WC2A 3ED

Alcohol Counselling Services
  34 Electric Lane
  London SW9 8JT
  071-737 3574

The Mantra Consultancy Group
  United House
  North Road,
  London N7 9DP
  071-609 9055

Westminster Pastoral Foundation
  23 Kensington Square
  London W8 5HN

*(London based, but branches all
  over the country)
  Industrial and group counselling.
  Long and short term therapeutic
  counselling.*

Relate
  76A New Cavendish Street
  London W1M 7LB
  071-580 1087/1088
  *Mainly marital but will deal with other
  issues.*

Alcoholics Anonymous
  London Office
  11 Redcliffe Gardens
  London SW10
  071-352 3001

Information and Social Services
  PO Box 1
  Stonebow House
  Stonebow
  York YO1 2NJ
  0904 644020

Release
  Criminal, Legal and Drugs Service
  169 Commercial Street
  London E1
  071-377 5905
  071-603 8654 (24 hr – helping)

SCODA
  Standing Conference On Drug Abuse
  1 Hatton Place
  London EC1
  071-430 2341

One-to-One Management

CEPEC
   Kent House
   41 East Street
   Bromley
   Kent BR1 1QQ
   081-464 1245
Trains in post-incident support –
   support for employees in banks,
   health service, prisons, police
   services, retailing, transport.

Appendix VI

Selected Reading

There are numerous books written on counselling. This is a selection which we have found useful.

1. Stress

Causes, Coping and Consequences of Stress at Work
Cary L Cooper and Roy Payne (eds)
Wiley, 1988

Living with Stress
Cary L Cooper, Rachel D Cooper and Lynn Eaker
Penguin, 1988

Pressure at Work : A Survival Guide
Tanya Arroba and Kim James
McGraw Hill, 1987

Social Skills and Mental Health
BM Bryant and M Argyle
Methuen, 1978

The Joy of Stress
Peter Hanson
Pan, 1987
pp. 7-95

2. General management

The Social Psychology of Work
Michael Argyle
Penguin, 1989

Process Consultation
E Schein
Addison-Wesley, 1969

Managing People at Work: A Manager's Guide to Behaviour in Organisations
John Hunt
McGraw Hill, 1986

Understanding Organisations
C B Handy
Penguin Books, 1976

3. Counselling skills

Counselling : A Practical Guide for Employers
Michael Megranaham
Institute of Personnel Management, 1989

Counselling People at Work : An Introduction for Managers
R de Board
Gower, 1983

Exercises in Helping Skills: A Training Manual to Accompany the Skilled Helper
Gerard Egan
Brooks Cole, 1985

Counselling in an Organisation
J D Dicken and F J Roethlisberger
Harvard University, 1966

On Becoming a Counsellor : A Basic Guide for Non-professional Counsellors
E Kennedy
Gill and Macmillan, 1977

Principles of Counselling
BBC Further Education
London, 1978

Practical Counselling Skills
R Nelson-Jones

4. General interpersonal skills

Psychology for Managers
  eds C L Cooper and P Makins. Chapter by B Hogan on 'Counselling and Helping'
  MacMillan, 1984

Radical Approaches to Social Skills Training
  P Tower ED
  Croom Helm, 1984

The Psychology of Interpersonal Behaviour
  M Argyle
  Penguin, 1970

On Becoming a Person
  C R Rogers
  Constable, 1961

Skills with People: A Guide for Managers
  E Sidney, M Brown and M Argyle
  Hutchinson, 1963

Games People Play
  E Berne
  Grove Press Inc, 1964
  Penguin, 1968

What Do You Say After You Say Hello?
  E Berne
  Bantam Books, 1973

Index